PRIVILEGE
AND BURDEN

BOOKS BY ROBERT G. MIDDLETON
Tensions in Modern Faith
Privilege and Burden

PRIVILEGE
AND BURDEN

Robert G. Middleton

JUDSON PRESS, VALLEY FORGE

for Evelyn

CONTENTS

PREFACE

"Everything nailed down is coming loose." Those words from *Green Pastures* provide a capsule description of our era. In virtually every field of endeavor, change has been the dominant experience. The pace of change in our era has been greatly increased, with a consequent experience of confusion and uncertainty. We are not sure where we are, sometimes not clear as to who we are, and quite adrift in regard to where we are heading.

No claim is made that the pastoral ministry is the only profession undergoing this kind of radical reappraisal; other professions are going through a similar searching. What is clear is that the ministry confronts a grave crisis of meaning and purpose. The pages of this book are my attempt to see where we now are and to indicate what seems to me a valid approach to the pastoral ministry in the light of the changes now taking place.

I have not attempted to minimize the radical nature of the challenge now facing the church and its ministry. This would be a foolish strategy and one doomed to failure. No ostrich-like hiding will do. Facing the changes directly, I want to affirm my belief, stronger now than at any time in my ministry, in the worth, the excitement, and the significance of the pastoral ministry. I hope that this comes through clearly in the chapters of the book.

There are two groups who have been particularly in my mind as I have written these chapters. One group is that represented by men of my own generation, roughly midway in their careers. Such men wonder now if there is a continuing validity in the pastoral ministry. As honestly as I know how, I have tried to face that question and to give what seems to me a satisfying answer. Of course, the future is going to be more difficult than the past has been; we are in for some rough times, and we had better reckon with that possibility. But if the Christian faith has a future, then the pastoral ministry also has a future. And since I believe that God has called a people to be his people in a particular way, summoning us to mission in the world for the sake of the Kingdom, I believe that the pastoral ministry is on the threshold of new significance. Accordingly, I hope that men of my generation may catch a new thrill in being "where the action really is" and rejoice in the pastoral vocation.

Also in mind has been a second group. This group is composed of young men, now committed to the Christian venture, but not at all sure that the pastorate is the place of service for them. Some signs indicate that the current group of seminarians may be over the anti-institutional kick and ready to look at the pastoral ministry with real seriousness. For such young men this book is an attempt to state honestly what the pastorate is like. If it reads once in a while like a recruiting manual, I am not worried; my intention, quite frankly, is to lay upon the brightest and keenest young men in the Christian community the possibility that the pastoral ministry may be a place of significance and challenge for them.

The greatest asset for a man in the pastoral ministry, I firmly believe, is a fine family; and in this I have been richly blessed. My sons — Robert, Douglas, Jeffrey, and David — have listened to many of my ideas and have helped to sharpen them, sometimes by agreeing, sometimes by disagreeing, but always forcing me to take into account the feelings of a younger generation. This book is dedicated to my wife, but such dedication is utterly inadequate to express my gratitude to her and for her. She has somehow managed to find time to type the manuscript of this book, in the midst of many other tasks, and to help in countless other ways. She has shared the privilege and the burden and made it all joy.

ROBERT G. MIDDLETON

1

THE SEEDS OF DISENCHANTMENT

Modern Protestantism is caught in a crisis of significant proportion. A widespread attack has been launched upon the institutional church. From within and from without the ranks of the church the indictment is thundered forth. Cries are raised that the organized church, as we have known it for a long time, is outmoded, irrelevant, and a hindrance to the spread of the gospel. One result of this attack is a vocational crisis felt by those in the ranks of the pastoral ministry. Their place of privilege and burden is more and more regarded as an anachronism in today's Christian witness. The exciting frontier of Christian action seems to be located anywhere but in the local congregation. As a result, young men preparing for the ministry are less attracted than ever to the pastoral care of a congregation, and men in the pastoral ministry are torn apart by perplexity about the worth and validity of their vocation.

The gravity of the situation was indicated by Eugene Carson Blake. Writing on the theme "The Church in the Next Decade," he first commented upon significant internal pressures upon the church. In this connection, Dr. Blake said that perhaps the most important internal pressure upon the churches stems from the confusion and frustration of the local pastor. . . . Some see in the flight from the pastorate merely a symptom of anti-institutionalism in the younger generation. Others see in it the obvious result of lay resistance to any leadership that would change the congregation from its nineteenth-century pattern. . . .

Neither of these reasons seemed sufficiently serious to account for the current crisis. Hence Dr. Blake went on to say that

there is a deeper cause than either of these. Too many pastors have failed to find any real theological connection between what is expected of them as preacher, pastor, and leader of a community of worship, on the one hand, and as a leader of relevant ethical and social change on the other. . . . And those who give up on the radical ethical drive of the Gospel break down under the pressures and irrelevancies of trying to be a professional chaplain to an essentially secular people.[1]

Such a judgment, coming from a man in close contact with Protestantism, may well set before us the extreme gravity of this crisis.

Anyone close to the current generation of seminary students realizes how sharp and profound is this crisis. The pastoral ministry simply does not attract the current generation as it did the past generation. This is not said in any judgmental sense. There are wonderful virtues in the current generation of seminary students. There is a bracing honesty about them, a resolute unwillingness to be content with easy and comfortable answers to probing questions. They are going to be "honest to God" and honest to their fellows. They are willing to wrestle with the tough questions. The seminary atmosphere is keen and exciting, and theology has a quality of adventure which it did not always possess in the past.

There is, however, an inescapable problem presented by

[1] Eugene Carson Blake, "The Church in the Next Decade," *Christianity and Crisis*, Vol. XXVI, No. 2 (February 21, 1966), p. 16. Copyright by Christianity and Crisis, Inc., 1966. Used by permission.

the desire of these young men to serve anywhere but in the pastoral ministry. Unless we give up entirely on the institutional church, unless we despair of the congregation completely, we must cherish the hope that some of these keen young men will give themselves to the pastoral ministry. At the present time, however, few of them seem really attracted to this place of service. If they consider the pastoral ministry at all, they usually see it as a temporary assignment, to be accepted until something more desirable opens up.

If a visitor were to question students at any ranking Protestant seminary, the conversation might well run like this:

Visitor: "Are you definitely committed to the ministry as a vocation?"

Student: "No, I am here essentially to explore the possibility."

Visitor: "What do you consider the basic task of the ministry?"

Student: "The basic task of the ministry, I believe, is to gossip the Gospel at a dimension of depth in such a way as to force the confrontation in genuine encounter with Christ which will in turn lead to an existential decision."

Visitor (somewhat overwhelmed by the preceding answer): "Are you thinking of the pastoral ministry?"

Student: "For God's sake" (literally), "no, indeed!"

I do not for a moment imply that every student in seminary would respond in such fashion. Fortunately, our seminaries are now training many young men for service in the parish ministry. This fact should be borne in mind, lest the picture become too distorted. But it is also evident that some of the keenest students, possessing many of the qualities needed in the pastoral ministry, have little or no interest in this area of service.

The barometer of statistics provides some readings to suggest that a storm is already here and possibly a worse storm is on the way. The enrollment in the 124 schools associated with the American Association of Theological

Schools has not shown any increase in the last several years. However, this failure to keep pace with the growing population is compounded by the decrease in the number of students choosing programs leading to the pastoral ministry. This number is down by 392 when compared with the number in such programs in 1961. At the same time, the number of students choosing programs leading to teaching positions is up by 286. These figures may be no cause for panic, but they are reason for concern. According to the recent Culver-Bridston report to the AATS (American Association of Theological Schools), in the year 1960 there were almost twenty thousand students in residence in theological seminaries. Of this group, 73 percent indicated that they did not intend to be in the pastoral ministry ten years after graduation.

To the outward indicator of statistics can be added an impressionistic feeling concerning the loss of attraction of the pastoral ministry. The local church has come under such searching judgment that we have reached a point where many are questioning the worth of a life spent in the service of this institution. After studying three years in classrooms where the church is subjected to a merciless examination, its weaknesses glaringly exposed and its irrelevance monotonously documented, students are told, "Now go out and spend yourselves in the service of this institution." They may be pardoned if they are less than enthusiastic about such a proposition.

The situation has reached the place where Walter Wagoner can say, with only slight exaggeration:

> Criticism of the whole structure and form of the Christian enterprise has reached such proportions on seminary campuses that one would suspect, if the church were unionized, that a general strike was about to be called. More than criticism, the mood spills over into petulance, and now and then comes close to self-hatred and other curious perversities.[2]

[2] Walter Wagoner, *Bachelor of Divinity* (New York: Association Press, 1963), p. 17.

Statistics plus impressions indicate, then, that a very difficult situation confronts the churches when they set about to enlist the next generation of clergymen for the pastoral ministry.

This is bad enough, but it isn't the end of the story. We must also face the fact that hosts of men now engaged in the pastoral ministry feel the same nagging doubts and engage in the same probing questioning concerning the worth and validity of their vocation. John B. Coburn entitled his book on the ministry *Minister: The Man in the Middle.* The title is intriguing, but a more fitting description, in the light of today's situation, might be *Minister: The Man in the Muddle.* To call the ministry a muddled profession is only a slightly less elegant way of calling it, as H. Richard Niebuhr did, "the perplexed profession." [3] Whether the proper term is muddle or perplexity, it is quite impossible to miss the fact that the ministry is filled with men undergoing a crisis of self-examination. Along with the self-examination, perhaps even stimulating the process, is an agonizing wrestling with the meaning of the church as expressed in its local parish reality.

The reality of this perplexity is visible in the articles which occupy considerable space in the mass-circulation magazines. Some years ago everyone became worried at the revelation of mental breakdown among Protestant ministers. There is rarely a year during which some magazine does not carry an article in which a man, pushed to the limit of his patience, tells "Why I Quit the Ministry." Several foundations have appropriated considerable sums of money to study one aspect or another of the problem of the contemporary minister. One study, ostensibly dealing with theological education, found it necessary to spend most of its time and a good share of its printed report on the state of the ministry, taking a look back to see the

[3] H. Richard Niebuhr, *The Purpose of the Church and Its Ministry* (New York: Harper & Row, Publishers, Inc., 1956), p. 48.

problem in perspective and a look within to see the problem in depth. The ministry today is "the perplexed profession" indeed.

When the minister has a sense of the worthwhileness of his ministry, he does not spend his time worrying about justifying the vocation to himself and to the laity. The hectic busyness which has so fragmented the ministry is a move of desperation, a rather pathetic attempt to stifle one's own questions and those of the laity. If a great deal of activity is going on all the time, and if, furthermore, this frenzied activity is pursued with a perpetually shining ecclesiastical smile, we are hopeful that this will serve as a substitute for a resolute attempt to do the job which needs to be done.

The difficulty of recruiting talented young men for the pastoral ministry and the fading sense of worth in their vocation felt by many who have served for some years in the pastoral ministry combine to indicate a third serious aspect of the current situation. The church becomes more and more ineffective. It seems that we are caught in a vicious circle. The irrelevance and the ineffectiveness of the church as it is now produce a situation in which young men no longer look to the pastorate as a place of real opportunity and challenge and create serious self-questioning on the part of men now in the pastorate. The result is that the ineffectiveness increases. If there is to be a renewal of the church in the future, we must recognize the urgent necessity of thinking through anew the meaning of the pastoral ministry. If this can be done in such fashion that the present defects of the churches serve as challenges calling out the best in ministers and not as excuses for abandoning the whole local church enterprise, we can hope for renewal. But without some solution to the problem of ministerial morale, we are going to be in for some exceedingly rough days ahead.

What has caused this present disenchantment? No full

treatment of the causes can be attempted within the bounds of this chapter, but I want to indicate some seeds of disenchantment which seem to be of real importance in bringing us to our present impasse.

It is not possible to isolate completely the problem of the ministry from the other problems confronting Christianity, especially American Protestant Christianity, in this day and age. There will be no solution to the problem of the ministry unless and until there is some sort of solution to these other problems which are part of the general Christian climate of opinion. We shall return to some of these problems later in this book, but the intention now is simply to identify them.

The contemporary Protestant minister faces reasons for disenchantment in three areas of his life and work. These three areas, I believe, are very important. They are far removed from the minor irritations and restrictions often advanced as reasons to explain "Why I Quit the Ministry." Any man who could be driven out of the ministry by some of these minor things probably should not be in the profession anyway. The three areas we want to explore, then, are fundamental to our present disenchantment. The minister is theologically confused, sociologically displaced, and vocationally perplexed. Any one of these alone would be serious enough; when all three are experienced at about the same time, the situation is filled with the potentiality of vocational crisis, as hosts of ministers, young and old, newcomers and veterans are now experiencing.

I

There is no question but that the general theological climate now prevailing contributes significantly to the disenchantment felt by men in the pastoral ministry. The current theological situation is difficult to describe. No single view is dominant enough to give its stamp to the whole venture of theological thinking. Perhaps the most that can be said is that this is an "interim period" theologically. But it is an interim period characterized by some of the deepest radical questioning seen in many decades. The current scene is sufficiently radical in its questioning of basic presuppositions to make the liberal movement of the recent past seem a rather timid venture.

This is not in any sense an attempt to judge the current trends, although a certain prejudice will probably show through what I am saying. The basic intention here is only to report on this tumult from the point of view of its impact on the mood and morale of men in the pastoral ministry.

To do this, I want to describe a bit more fully two specific emphases of the current theological scene, both of which seem to embody a threat to the morale of the pastoral ministry. The two emphases are very closely linked, the one depending upon and implying the other.

The first is the movement, associated with some fragments from Dietrich Bonhoeffer's prison correspondence, to develop what can only be called an atheistic Christianity. The catchy slogan of the movement is that "God is dead." The important passage from Bonhoeffer is in the letter of July 16, 1944, where he writes:

> There is no longer any need for God as a working hypothesis, whether in morals, politics or science. Nor is there any need for such a God in religion or philosophy (Feuerbach). In the name of intellectual honesty these working hypotheses should be dropped or dispensed with as far as possible. . . .
> So our coming of age forces us to a true recognition of our situation *vis a vis* God. God is teaching us that we must live as men who can get along very well without him. . . . The God who makes us live in this world without using him as a working hypothesis is the God before whom we are ever standing. Before God and with him we live without God.[4]

[4] Dietrich Bonhoeffer, *Letters and Papers from Prison* (New York: The Macmillan Company, 1962), pp. 218-219.

This contention of Bonhoeffer has been picked up and used by a number of theologians of the contemporary scene. While they cleave to some aspects of the Christian tradition, they forsake any belief in God. The God of the Christian tradition, as conventionally interpreted, is dead as far as these writers are concerned.

It is not hard to imagine the effect of this type of theological thinking upon the man in the pastoral ministry. Not only as preacher but also as pastor, he finds it necessary to help people to find a sustaining faith in the midst of a perplexing world. This task is always difficult, and the minister who is worthy of his calling does not seek any exemption from the anguish of searching for meaning. Nevertheless, the "God is dead" theology strikes many men in the pastoral ministry as being curiously irrelevant, even silly. If this is all that a man can say about God in this day and age, it must be accepted as an honest statement. But such a statement gives very little real guidance and offers no real light upon man's fundamental problem with the ultimate meanings in life.

The result of this kind of emphasis, whatever its general validity, is to raise serious questions in the minds of many men about the importance of the church, either local or universal, in a day when all that the church seemingly has to teach is a wistful veneration of the figure of Jesus. The task of the minister is sufficiently difficult at best; it becomes for many an utterly impossible calling on the basis of an assumption that "God is dead."

Closely related to this concept of the "death of God" is a second emphasis; indeed, this second emphasis seems a logical development of the first. If man can no longer depend upon God, since God is dead, he must face the fact that man has finally come of age. He has been emancipated from his infantile dependence upon God and, in the proud assertion of modern culture and technology, he is now on his own. The guidance once sought in religion is cast aside. He now has only himself to depend upon. For good or ill, he will make his own world.

Back of this emphasis upon a "world-come-of-age" there is an impressive historical development. Through the years, the self-reliance of man has been growing. The restless probing of man's mind has brought one area after another under his control. Where a former age sought to retain God as an explanation of the mysteries which remained, man today finds such a hypothesis increasingly irrelevant. The idea of any dependence upon God is rejected as being a little silly. Man has grown up, say these people, and no longer has any need for God.

The result of this thinking is the development of an approach to the secular which is a significant change from the assessment popular a few short years ago. Secularism was then regarded very widely as the chief enemy of the Christian faith, and it stood for the organization of life apart from God as though God did not exist. Now, however, the secular has become the precise area wherein Christian witness is to be carried on. Far from being a danger, we are called to a "holy worldliness," and any insistence that there is a tension between the church and the world is highly suspect. Any feeling that there is a sharp distinction between church and world is simply a carryover from an earlier day. We are to be secularists, and we are to rejoice in our secularity.

In passing, it is a strange commentary on our Christian vitality that we should have chosen to secularize the sacred instead of invading the secular with the sacred. Perhaps there is in this an implied judgment upon the Christian community: we lacked sufficient confidence boldly to claim the secular in the name of the sacred. Our weakness of conviction may have led us to hand over the sacred to be swallowed up in the secular.

A later chapter will make plain our conviction that the Christian must be in deep sympathy with much of the

emphasis on "holy worldliness." The bothersome aspect of
the secular emphasis, however, is the question about the
significance of the Christian community. As far as the minister is concerned, it sometimes seems that in the maintenance of the local congregation he is actually doing something which is a direct hindrance to the Christian enterprise. The invitation to people to share in the life of the
church becomes a diversion, according to some, from the
real Christian task of working in the world. Obviously, the
problem here is one of balance; a good part of the current
difficulty arises from a failure to hold in a living balance
the emphases upon the church gathered and the church
scattered. Much of the current literature critical of the
church is eloquent in its emphasis upon the scattered people of God; it is hesitant and almost embarrassed about the
activities of the gathered community. No doubt this is
partly to be welcomed as the redressing of the lack of
balance in the past, and the usual phenomenon is here observed: the reaction itself goes too far and needs in turn
to be brought into balance.

However, this lack of any emphasis upon the validity of
the gathered church, its life as a community of worship,
mission, and fellowship, undermines the morale of the minister. He not only feels that he has lost the thrill of being
in a place of pivotal importance in terms of the purpose
of God, but he suffers from a feeling of guilt produced by
spending time and effort on maintaining an institution
which is so far removed from the important realm of secular witness.

II

In addition to this theological confusion, the Protestant
minister is sociologically a displaced person today. It is
clear that American society has gone through a significant
revolution in the past few years. For a good part of our

national history, life in the United States was pretty well dominated by what E. Digby Baltzell has called "The Protestant Establishment." [5] The real source of power in society was located in this group, sometimes popularly referred to as WASPS (white, Anglo-Saxon Protestants). The members of this Establishment dominated for many decades the political, economic, and intellectual life in America.

It is very evident now that the days of the Protestant Establishment are over. Nor is this something to mourn about. We have moved into a pluralistic society. We may have moved into what is called a post-Protestant period. Certainly, we have emerged into an entirely new sort of setting. The unquestioned self-assurance of the Protestant, confident that he runs the nation, is a thing of the past. Now he lives and works and shares power with the Catholic, the Jew, and the host of Americans who profess no religious faith whatever.

This revolution — and it *is* a revolution even if a quiet one — has not been without its effect upon the Protestant minister. However, it would be extremely naive to imagine that the minister of the past figured very largely or very influentially in the deliberations of the Establishment. Even in the past, he was likely to be looked upon as a sort of harmless being, maintained by the Establishment to lend an aura of sanctity to the making of decisions which needed something to make them seem honorable. It is the contention of Professor Baltzell that the last Protestant clergyman to hold a position of real influence, such that his words and opinions would be respected both among business men and by union labor, was Bishop Henry Cadman Potter. But few of the ministers in the days of the Protestant Establishment's smug confidence had the power of a Bishop Potter.

Nevertheless, if realism compels this admission, the Prot-

[5] E. Digby Baltzell, *The Protestant Establishment* (New York: Random House, 1964).

estant minister of the past did have a secure place in the society of his day. He knew where he belonged. He had his proper niche. He was not, sociologically speaking, a displaced person. Even if he judged the Establishment as a prophet, he knew that finally he was part of that group; and he also knew that his place was secure.

This change can be put in terms of a picture, admittedly trivial, but symptomatic of what has taken place. Imagine a town or small city somewhere in the United States — north, east, south, or west matters little — several decades ago. A ceremonial occasion is at hand. A prayer is to be offered to open the civic ceremonies. To perform this ritualistic bow to God a Protestant minister will be asked to sit on the front row with other civic dignitaries. He is part of the ruling group, a member of the Establishment at least in terms of social location. He has his place; it is known by him and by others, and hence he has the quiet assurance of being to some degree a member of the power elite of his community.

Imagine now a similar gathering today. There may still be a prayer offered, since old rituals cling rather tenaciously. But the chances are fairly good that the prayer will not be offered by a Protestant pastor. Certainly, in many American communities the choice is no longer automatic. What has happened is that two others have come along, tapped the Protestant pastor on the shoulder and said, with great goodwill and also with a sense of having waited quite a while, "Move over, brother, we are going to sit with you." And the Jewish rabbi and Roman Catholic priest sit down. One other change has occurred in the civic seating arrangements. All three — minister, priest, and rabbi — now sit in an inconspicuous back row.

Obviously, this imaginary picture would not hold true everywhere. There are many areas of the country where the Protestant Establishment still holds the reins of actual power and the Protestant pastor continues to have an assured position. But the *trend* is in this direction of the ending of the exclusive power of the Protestant Establishment, and this trend is likely to be accelerated in the immediate future.

Let me repeat here what was said in beginning this phase of our discussion: this whole course of development is good. Far from being a matter about which the Protestant community should shake its collective head in despair, this development should be welcomed. When properly understood, it is a liberating movement. It provides the chance for the Protestant church to take its proper place as the servant community. Instead of rejoicing in its power, the church is freed to glory in its servanthood. There should be no misunderstanding at this point. The passing of the Protestant Establishment is noted here with joy more than with nostalgia.

When, however, we attempt to list the factors which have gone into the shaping of the ministerial disenchantment of the present and the recent past, this factor must be included. The man in the Protestant ministry today has lost the sense of security which came from an assured social position, and this very assurance had helped maintain his morale even during periods when he may have had grave inner questionings about the real validity of his vocation. Now the Protestant minister faces the difficult task of adjusting to a new sociological place at the same time that he faces theological tumult and confusion.

III

Thus far we have said that the disenchantment of the minister has been produced by theological confusion and sociological displacement. Now we must confront the disenchantment produced by vocational perplexity.

The basic trouble is a loss of identity on the part of

the minister.[6] He is simply not at all sure what his true function is supposed to be. This confusion attends the minister in his role within the church and also touches his role as the spokesman of the church in its relation to society and culture. Nowhere does the minister today find a clear and compelling understanding of his task.

The image of the minister which is presented to sensitive observers is caught in part of Richard Chase's *The Democratic Vista:*

> Yes, the preacher loses all sense of dignity and of a sacred calling, and tends to become a combination ethical counselor, social worker, psychotherapist, group organizer, and Rotarian booster. The lay proselytizers who try to get you to join their church always tell you that their minister is a "straight-from-the-shoulder" type and that there is no nonsense about *him,* meaning, of course, *no religion.* As for the clergyman himself, he has no time for religion, even if he is so inclined. He is one of the army of the underpaid and overworked on whom a thoughtless and childlike society unloads its personal problems.[7]

The accuracy of this picture can be verified by introspection on the part of the average Protestant minister. He is indeed perplexed as he confronts the mysterious and challenging meaning of his calling. The tragic nature of the situation is to be found in the fact that the minister often has an image of himself and his calling which is quite at odds with what seems to be demanded of him. The modern minister, perhaps more than the clergyman of any other period, finds himself driven by a variety of pressures into a mold he neither chooses for himself nor be-

[6] This section with minor editorial revisions is taken from my article, "Let the Minister Be a Minister," *Foundations,* Vol. II (July, 1959), pp. 198ff.

[7] Richard Chase, *The Democratic Vista: A Dialogue on Life and Letters in Contemporary America* (New York: Doubleday & Company, Inc., 1958), p. 121. Copyright © 1958 by Richard Chase. Reprinted by permission of Doubleday & Company, Inc.

lieves to be the proper one for the minister. Such a situation sets up within the minister a tension which reduces his effectiveness and hampers the witness of the church.

The image of the ministry which is shared by hosts of clergymen is that of the minister as a man of God. But he cannot be a man of God in isolation; he is called to be a man of God in the midst of the believing community. He is to be the servant of the church, and consequently to find his true role as that of one person in the total body of believers, all of whom are ministers. His is the task of the professional, using that term in its best and highest sense, to endeavor to deal helpfully with the spiritual problems of the modern man.

The church, seen in this way, does not exist for the minister; he exists for the church. His functions are to be exercised within the life of the community of the faithful. By dint of careful study and spiritual discipline, the minister is to help perplexed men and women to know the deep things of God. It is in this area, then, that the minister sees his basic task. He is to be a man of God in the life of the believing community.

But such a description of the ministry is obviously an idealized portrait, bearing little if any resemblance to what the harried modern minister must actually do. To carry out the task outlined here would demand more of the minister than he could possibly deliver. But even to approach the task of the ministry in this way is rendered quite impossible because this image of the ministry is at odds with the image of the ministry held in many instances by the laity and, as a result, taken over by many ministers as well.

It is important, therefore, to stress that the working out of the problem of the ministry today is not alone the responsibility of the minister or of the theological seminary or of groups financed by generous philanthropists. All of these are involved, to be sure, and their help is needed.

But the task is basically one which confronts the church itself. Ministry and laity together, as members of the believing community, must address themselves afresh to the question of the basic nature and function of the Christian church. When this has been done, we shall be in a position to see properly the task of the ministry.

Consequently, we have a long, long way to go before the present confusion regarding the ministry can be cleared up. This confusion exists in the minds of the laity. When a pulpit committee is asked, "What are the qualities you want in your minister, and what do you expect of him?" their answers demonstrate the fact that most churches have little idea of the basic function of the Christian minister. What they want their minister to be and to do is often far removed from what he conceives his real task to be.

The churches are frequently, if not always, anxious to find in the minister qualities which he regards at best as peripheral to his work as a minister of the gospel. To confront such demands again and again raises in the mind of the minister anxious questions about his own image of his task. Unless his image is a very strong one indeed, he may soon come to the conclusion that he must have been wrong and that his job is to be and to do what the people of the churches want him to be and to do. Thus, confusion existing in the life of the church creeps into the life of the minister as well.

This is particularly a peril for a minister in the Free Church tradition, for the life of such a minister is bound up with the people of the church. If he is a humble man, he may feel it arrogant on his part to insist stubbornly on a conception of the ministry which the laity of the churches seem quite clearly to have rejected. It is both more humble and a great deal easier to adjust his own image of his calling to fit the expectations of the people to whom he is bound in faith and love.

The picture of the type of minister desired by the

churches is furnished in the Hartshorne-Froyd study of some years ago dealing with ministers of the American Baptist fellowship. Although the study was made in 1944, there is no ground for assuming that the ideas have changed greatly since that time. One part of the study, based upon the replies of some seventy-eight laymen, sought to discover the qualities desired in a minister. The resulting list is dismaying indeed, as examples will show. Among the personal qualities desired, the most important is that the minister be a good mixer with young and old. This rates far above the desire for a minister who would be alert, intelligent, and progressive. It ranks far ahead of the desire for a minister who would be humble and courteous. Indeed, the top three qualities are all in the same realm: a good mixer, sociable and agreeable, and a pleasing personality. The spiritual qualities desired are described in traditional terms of devotion to Christian calling and service to God. These stand ahead of a working knowledge of the Bible and the quality of love of God and man. Among leadership qualities, skill in teaching and leading children and youth ranks ahead of being a good pastor. Very near the bottom of the list is the quality of fearlessness in presenting the message of the gospel. After reading through such a table, which reflects the confusion in the minds of the laity, it is easy to understand the statement of the authors: "If what the churches say they want should be taken as the basis of theological education, the clock would have to be turned back a hundred years." [8]

There can be no question that there is confusion in the minds of the laity about the nature and function of the Christian minister. Despite this, it would be wrong to place the blame for the contemporary situation upon the layman.

[8] Hugh Hartshorne and Milton Froyd, *Theological Education in the Northern Baptist Convention* (Valley Forge: The Judson Press, 1945), p. 52.

Minister and layman alike have shared a common outlook, one in which the conception of the nature and function of the ministry is approached more from the viewpoint of contemporary society than from the perspective of biblical faith. Here is the root of the problem: our idea of the ministry is determined not so much by the insights of faith as by the standards of a predominantly secular society.

The real nature of the problem was easily overlooked at a time when the institutions of religion seemed vital and full of life. In the midst of a widespread turning to "religion," we have thought all was well. The buildings went up and so did the budgets. The activities expanded. The membership rolls grew larger and larger. We showed all the signs of vigor and vitality. Religion seemed to be a success in modern America during the fifties. The ministry found itself pervaded by the success mentality which is so much a part of the American outlook. The result of having hosts of new members in the churches may well have been the further secularization of the church, until the church became virtually indistinguishable from the rest of society. And, by the same subtle process, the minister became no different from many other helpful persons in modern society.

Now that the statistical measures of success have begun to turn downward, the emotional force of the problem of the role of the minister is felt much more strongly. In the midst of the disenchantment now so evident among ministers, there is a tendency to seek the proper concept of the minister's role anywhere but in the insights of the Christian tradition. The minister, lacking any clear concept of his proper function, is easily molded into any shape desired. At the same time that this process is going on, however, the minister is disturbed by misgivings about the whole thing. Somewhere, he feels, he has lost his proper self; what he now recognizes himself to be is not at all what he really wanted to be at the start of his career. It is not what he wants at those moments when he is most sensitively aware of his calling's authentic task. No matter how deep his misgivings may go, the minister knows that his calling has changed rather drastically. An illustration of this which would be amusing if it were not so tragic is provided by Gereon Zimmerman in an article dealing with the problem not only of the minister but of the priest and rabbi as well. Mr. Zimmerman writes:

> In drawing up a psychological test for seminaries for the Rockefeller Brothers program, the Educational Testing Service sent a questionnaire to 1,000 lay leaders in various denominations, asking them to mention adjectives and to give profiles that represented their own concept of "an outstanding minister." This data was then turned over to another group of psychological testers, who were not told who was being described. These testers were asked, "Who do you think is being described?" Their answer: "A junior vice-president of Sears-Roebuck." [9]

Such a response is simply a particularly telling bit of evidence to support the contention of this section: the contemporary minister is facing a situation of acute vocational perplexity. He simply does not know who he really is and therefore does not really know what he is supposed to be doing.

There has been a process of disenchantment with the pastoral ministry. Surely, this process has gone on long enough to become a major concern of the Christian church. The theological confusion, sociological displacement, and vocational perplexity which have produced the disenchantment must be faced squarely.

What has made this task so difficult is that while this process has been going on, creating the sort of problem we have attempted to sketch in this chapter, another enterprise has also been under way. A host of people have been taking

[9] Gereon Zimmerman, "Help Wanted: Ministers, Priests and Rabbis," *Look*, November 20, 1962, p. 117.

a very hard look at the church. Some of these people are theologians, some are sociologists, some are believers, and others are nonbelievers. Any man who seeks to serve in the pastoral ministry must, I believe, undergo the discipline of looking at the church through the eyes of such critics. Such a hard look at the church is what we shall attempt in the next chapter.

2

A HARD LOOK
AT THE CHURCH

In his book *Life Is Commitment* J. H. Oldham tells of a luncheon he had many years ago in London with Paul Tillich. On that occasion, he said to his friend, "You know, Tillich, Christianity has no meaning for me whatsoever apart from the Church, but I sometimes feel as though the Church as it actually exists is the source of all my doubts and difficulties."[1] The statement sums up not only the feeling of a perceptive theologian and devoted servant of the church, but the attitude of an increasing number of people within the church and outside it. It comes very close to an accurate summation of the feeling of many now in the parish ministry. The dilemma of the ministry comes to focus in such a statement: Christianity unthinkable without the church; Christianity hampered in its expression by the present structure of the church.

The past few decades have seen the tempo of criticism of the present structure of the church steadily mounting. A veritable barrage has been directed at the church, especially at the church in its local expression. Accusations have been

[1] Joseph H. Oldham, *Life Is Commitment* (New York: Harper & Row, Publishers, Inc., 1952), p. 79.

hurled at the churches, clearly implying that the churches as they now exist are a positive hindrance to the effective propagation of the Christian faith.

I

This criticism has had its effect upon the men who are in the parish ministry. Facing this barrage of hostile critics, the parish minister adopts one of several approaches.

Some ministers have a built-in mechanism by which to dodge the force of contemporary criticism. They have so largely forsaken any serious study that they are not even aware of the fact of the criticism. They are caught up in the harmless diversions of ecclesiastical life. Entranced by the spectacle of parish wheels in motion, they never even stop to question whether or not all the motion adds up to anything significant. They have been trained in the traditional concept of the minister's proper role to be a dutiful servant of the institution. What's good for the institution, they are convinced, is good for them; they find in this conception the whole point and purpose of their ministry.

To become sarcastic and caustic about such ministers would be neither compassionate nor constructive. Ministers like these are rather tragic figures. They are quaint survivals in the twentieth century of forms of church life and existence proper for the nineteenth century. Victims of the snail's pace by which the church changes, they should be more pitied than scorned. They are losing out in the exciting ventures of today's Christian witness. They are living in a day which calls for some revolutionary changes in the church, but they are quite unaware of this fact.

There are other ministers, however, who at least know that this sort of criticism is being directed at the churches they serve. They cannot ignore the barrage. The shots are landing all around them, some with a dull thud, others with a brilliant pyrotechnic display. Since they are forcibly reminded at frequent intervals of all this shooting, they must take some position.

The answer of this group is a defensive counterattack. Unable for the most part to admit the validity of any of the criticism, they lodge an attack upon the attackers. Who, they ask, are the men who write the books and articles in which the attacks are largely made? Answering their own question, they point out that these men are usually professors in theological seminaries or else bureaucrats from some niche of the ecumenical movement. From this observation it is only a short step to the next barrage in the counterattack: professors are noted for being "theoretical" and ecumenical bureaucrats are known to be "impractical." Few of these critics are at the grass-roots level (beloved phrase!) and hence they inhabit "ivory towers" far removed from any contact with real people or real institutions. They don't really know the needs of the churches; their heads are in the clouds of abstraction. Let them use their brains to show the minister how he can raise the church budget and more efficiently organize his church. That would be a real service, and it would not be a hodgepodge of egg-headed theory.

Ministers who are neither blind to the problem nor defensive about the church as it now is react to the indictment of the institutional church in another way. They take the criticism so seriously that their morale is shattered. Unable to see the chinks in the armor of the critics, they accept at full value *all* of the charges. Instead of a careful process of discriminating judgment, carefully weighing the charges to determine what is valid and what is invalid in the indictment, there is a complete acceptance of the charges. The result is a loss of morale. If the institutional church is so bad, there can be no hope for it, and the only proper response is either to leave a sinking ship or to sacrifice the thrill and zest once known in the vocation. Either result is tragic in consequences, both for the church and for the individual minister.

Happily, however, there is a fourth approach possible to all the attacks upon the church. This is a *dedicated openness*. It would be foolish to pretend that this is an easy approach to develop or to maintain. On the contrary, it is exceedingly hard to keep from falling into any of the other possible approaches we have sketched briefly. By dedicated openness I mean, first of all, a basic commitment to the church of Jesus Christ. This is a commitment made to the church as the body of Christ, the people of God, the fellowship of the Spirit. Essential to this commitment is a conviction that the Christian venture must have some form and structure through which the basic witness is carried on. Once this sort of commitment has been made, a man must realize that it is immature folly to imagine that the Christian mission can be effectively carried on without some form or structure.

This dedication does not call for an unthinking acceptance of everything as it exists in the church. Nevertheless, we today enjoy the benefits of the Christian faith because in the past some of the structures we now condemn so harshly existed and transmitted the faith from one generation to another. In saying this, I am not for a moment arguing that because this function has been fulfilled in the past we should therefore abdicate the responsibility of judging the church of the present, not at all. What I am suggesting is that if there is a peril for the church in a hardening of ancient practices until they no longer serve as vehicles for the work of God's Spirit, there is also a danger that the radical innovators may be blind to any possible values in the procedures of the past. Very little in terms of constructive alternatives seems to have emerged as yet from all the attacks on what is now being done. It is intellectual child's play to point out what is wrong in current procedures in the church; it is much more demanding to present a constructive alternative. An illustration of this sort of thing is provided by Colin Williams. He attacks much of our current practice in two little books, entitled, respectively, *Where in the World?* and *What in the World?* and then tries to duck out of the much harder job of telling *how in the world* the task of the church may be fulfilled.

So much, then, for the matter of dedication. By openness I mean a genuine willingness to listen attentively and even appreciatively to what the critics of the church are saying. It does not matter whether such critics speak from inside or outside the Christian community. No matter what the source of their insight, they should be listened to by all who believe in the church. Criticism will never kill the church; complacency can. While there may well be risk in taking seriously the hostile critics of the church, there is greater risk in sitting back and feeling that the church is somehow different from any other form of human organization in that it is beyond any criticism. This assumption makes the perilous error of identifying the church with the kingdom of God — and the tragic results of such an identification are written in some of history's sorriest pages. It is, therefore, far better to listen to what is said in judgment upon the church. The renewal of the church will come, we can be sure, only after the hard look has been taken. We must try, then, to combine a spirit of dedication with an attitude of openness.

In his helpful book *Self-Renewal: The Individual and the Innovative Society,* John W. Gardner deals basically with the renewal of the individual. He describes the qualities which are necessary in the individual who seeks renewal. These are also, I believe, the qualities needed in the modern ministry. He suggests the quality of openness, about which we have already had something to say, and goes on to suggest *independence* and in connection with this quality writes: "The creative individual has the capacity to free himself from the web of social pressures in which the rest of us are caught. . . . He is capable of questioning assumptions that the rest of us accept." Moreover, this person "is particularly gifted in seeing the gap between what *is* and what *could be* (which means, of course, that he has achieved a certain measure of detachment from what *is*)."[2] The other attributes mentioned are *flexibility,* a much needed quality in equipping the church for its mission; and *a capacity to find order in experience,* which is essential if, out of the welter of criticisms of the form of the church, we are to emerge with some clear and compelling visions of what ought to be. Perhaps our possession of some of these qualities will be demonstrated best by our willingness to take "a hard look at the church," using for this purpose the eyes of the contemporary critics of the church.

In what follows in this chapter, then, an attempt will be made to state accurately and honestly what the critics are saying. To accomplish this, we shall attempt to get inside the critic's viewpoint and expound it as though it were our own. We can turn in later pages of this book to the task of evaluating what is valid or invalid in the judgments.

There is an embarrassing abundance of materials on hand. The problem is one of selection; we must try to choose out of all the criticisms those which seem to have the greatest validity. Accordingly, I want to lift out certain broad indictments and then let one or two critics illustrate the general drift of the charge. Perhaps three broad categories can be discerned.

First, there are the anti-institutionalists. The history of the church has been, according to these critics, a progressive decline from the intensity of the *Ecclesia* of the New Testament, primarily a fellowship in the Holy Spirit made known in Jesus Christ, to the institutionalism of the present-day church. This view will be illustrated in classic form by Emil Brunner.

[2] John W. Gardner, *Self-Renewal: The Individual and the Innovative Society* (New York: Harper & Row, Publishers, Inc., 1963), p. 36; the discussion of the qualities necessary for renewal is found on pages 35-40.

Second, there are those who, although they do not condemn all institutions, see no hope for the traditional, resi-
dentially-oriented parish or church. This view is set forth in
its best-known form by Gibson Winter.

Third, there are those who indict the church as it now
is for ethical irrelevance and timid conformity. We shall
listen in this connection to Peter Berger and to an outsider,
the late C. Wright Mills, who was a sociologist and a man
of passionate social sympathies.

II

No other agency finds itself judged by standards so
rigorous as those under which the churches stand. The ve-
hemence of the judgment is rooted in the church's own
calling. The failure of the church is seen to be so great
precisely because the commitment is so lofty. Very often,
the starting point for such a judgment is a certain disenchantment with what the church is now doing. From this
awareness of something radically wrong, the course of investigation leads back ever farther into the church's history
in an attempt to determine where the church took the fatal
wrong turn.

A stimulating attempt to make this sort of determination
is found in Emil Brunner's book *The Misunderstanding of
the Church*. His aim is renewal and his method is historical-
theological investigation. But his point of departure is a
concern born out of a sense of the failure of the church. He
puts his concern in this way:

> During the whole course of its history, by reason of the fact that
> it was essentially a collective rather than a fellowship, the Church
> has not only neglected to create a true brotherhood in Christ, but
> in many ways has positively hindered such a development. Yet, just
> here lies the essence of the New Testament *Ecclesia* — the oneness
> of communion with Christ by faith and brotherhood in love. . . .
> With or without the churches, if necessary even in opposition to
> them, God will cause the *Ecclesia* to become a real community of
> brothers. Whether the churches yield to this recognition or on the

contrary blind themselves to it will determine the question whether or not they have a future.[3]

Beginning with this concern growing out of the failure of the church to demonstrate in its life a real fellowship, Brunner asks the inevitable question: What happened to change the New Testament *Ecclesia,* a fellowship with Christ in the Holy Spirit, into the institutional church known through the centuries?

The answer is easy enough to state, though the process of development is intricate and hard to trace. The basic failure, the prime cause for all the other failures which have followed in its way, is a loss of the reality of the church as a fellowship of persons. Brunner's basic thesis is that the church "is essentially a fellowship of persons and not an institution." [4] He further says:

> The Church — firstly the early catholic, then the neo-catholic Roman church — is distinguished from the *Ecclesia* above all in this — that it is no longer primarily a communion of persons, but rather an institution, and — particularly in its Roman Catholic form — understands itself as such.[5]

The tragedy of the church, then, consists in losing the original power possessed by the New Testament *Ecclesia* to be a community of persons, and the gradual development in its place of a vast institutional apparatus.

It cannot be too strongly stressed that a serious departure from the New Testament *Ecclesia* takes place whenever the "fellowship of persons" is forgotten. The church, according to this point of view, cannot be a communion of persons and at the same time be an institution, for "as the Body of Christ it has nothing to do with an organization and has nothing of the character of the institutional about it."[6]

[3] Emil Brunner, *The Misunderstanding of the Church,* trans. by Harold Knight (Philadelphia: The Westminster Press, 1953), p. 118. Copyright © 1953, by W. L. Jenkins. Used by permission.

[4] *Ibid.,* p. 58.

[5] *Ibid.,* p. 74.

[6] *Ibid.,* p. 11.

This departure from the ideal began about the end of the first century. The fellowship founded by Christ — what Brunner calls the *Ecclesia* — was without any kind of regular officers, any sort of hierarchical order, and it had very little in the way of organization. It was, consequently, a fellowship of persons held together by Christ through the Holy Spirit. Brunner argues that the charge that such a lack of structure could lead only to anarchy can be levied only by one:

> upon whose mind the later juridical administration of the Church has left such an indelible imprint that he can imagine no other sort of order except that. But it is the mystery of the *Ecclesia* as the fellowship of the Spirit that it has an articulate living order without being legally organized.[7]

According to this line of reasoning to try to organize this fellowship, to inject into its dynamic quality of human relationships the elements of order and law, is to kill the very quality of life for which the *Ecclesia* exists.

But this is precisely what happened. Although the change from *Ecclesia* to church was not inevitable, according to Brunner, it is possible to point to certain conditions which together caused the change. The first was a response to the challenge of the gnostic heresies which threatened the *Ecclesia* with disruption and then with destruction. Consequently, Brunner explains, it became necessary for the *Ecclesia* to establish a canon of apostolic writings and a firm rule of faith, which became a creedal standard. In order to establish and enforce these two safeguards, the church also had to create an authoritative office, that of bishop.[8]

A second factor in the change was simply the growth in the number of members of the Christian fellowship. The pneumatic-charismatic order typical of primitive Christian-

[7] *Ibid*, p. 51.
[8] *Ibid.*, pp. 87-88.

ity was possible only as long as the *Ecclesia* was small. With the growth in numbers there came a need to try to keep secure this quality of Spirit-filled existence. Moreover, there was a need to regularize the life of the community. To depend only upon the Holy Spirit becomes too precarious for a sizable group of people. Thus, in the attempt to secure the living Word of God, theology and dogma are developed; the attempt to perpetuate a fellowship leads to the formation of an institution; and faith is replaced by a creed. These things can be manipulated, but the Holy Spirit cannot be so handled.[9]

The third factor producing the change was the waning of the eschatological expectation. A fellowship which believed earthly existence would very shortly terminate had little need of institutional forms and structures. When this expectation collapsed and a long historical existence was anticipated, some institutional forms and structures had to be devised.

As a result of the play of these three factors — and with the growth of sacramentalism as a vital, even primary factor — the *Ecclesia* changed into the church. The fellowship became an institution.

This development was not merely a change in degree, but in kind. A fundamental alteration took place when the *Ecclesia* changed into the church. This change is "a transformation rather than a development, because the essential being of the *Ecclesia* as a spiritual unity, a communion of persons, has in the process been wrought into something else — an institution." [10]

Brunner thus argues that this change represents a loss, not a gain; and during the centuries of the existence of the church and its institutional forms there has been a serious distortion of what was evidently intended in the beginning in the primitive Christian community. Despite this loss,

[9] *Ibid.*, p. 53.
[10] *Ibid.*, p. 83.

however, the church is not to be either despised or rejected. While it has not fulfilled the role it was intended to fulfill — to be a community of persons in Jesus Christ guided in their lives by the Holy Spirit — it has served as a protective shell within which the precious kernel of the *Ecclesia* could lodge. The churches both protect and conceal the *Ecclesia*. Thus, Brunner warns that there "can never be a question of deriving from this distinction between the *Ecclesia* and the Church a merely negative judgment upon or a hostile attitude toward the latter. A means which the providence of God has used for so long and to such powerful effect, must not be allowed to fall a victim to destructive criticism."[11] Though this is a responsible statement, it can hardly be denied that the basic impact of Emil Brunner's argument in *The Misunderstanding of the Church* is to cast serious doubt upon the validity of the institutional church.

Given this sort of conviction or bias, it is not at all surprising to find Emil Brunner attracted to a contemporary movement which endeavors to get rid of the institutional accretions and back to a pristine fellowship of persons in Jesus Christ. The movement is the Mukyokai or Non-Church movement in Japan. Here is the outline of what the Christian fellowship might be like if we could divest the church of its institutional character.

In a volume of essays published in tribute to Paul Tillich, Emil Brunner describes briefly this Non-Church movement and expresses his enthusiasm for it. The Non-Church movement grew out of the work of the greatest Japanese evangelist, Kaizo Utschimura, but did not begin in earnest until after the death of the great evangelist. Following his conversion to the Christian faith by an American missionary, Kaizo Utschimura and some other students founded a separate church. Never did the movement win a tremendous number of converts, but it was unusual in the quality of

[11] *Ibid.,* pp. 116-117.

the converts won and in their lasting fidelity to his principles. Three aspects of the Non-Church movement need to be stressed in order to make clear its anti-institutional stance.

The heart of the Non-Church Movement is found in hundreds of Bible-study groups. The Bible is the center of this movement, and much of the effort of those involved is directed toward the movement's particular kind of Bible study. In many, if not in all of the groups, it is necessary to know the biblical languages so that the Bible can be studied in Greek and Hebrew. Along with this direct study, however, there goes the printing of periodicals, commentaries, Greek synopses and concordances, and other such helpful materials. The actual groups vary in size. Some are quite large, varying from three or four hundred down to just a few. The groups meet on Sunday mornings in halls rented for the purpose or in homes. As described by Brunner, "The leader interprets the Bible in a kind of continuous sermon, and says the prayers. The 'congregation' sings and silently prays with him. This is their service."[12] There is no attempt made to deal with subtle theological questions. It is the Bible which is the focal point of their interest; and Brunner denies the claim made by others that the approach is basically fundamentalist. "The Bible as it is," says Brunner, " — and not man's thoughts about it — is, in their intent, to be taken for its value."[13]

A second feature is that the Non-Church movement is totally and completely a movement of laity. There are no paid ministers; there are no theologically trained ministers. Those who take the responsibility of leading the groups have other full-time professions; this is a witness, a service,

[12] Emil Brunner, "A Unique Christian Mission: The Mukyokai ('Non-Church') Movement in Japan," in *Religion and Culture,* Walter Leibrecht, ed. (New York: Harper & Row, Publishers, Inc., 1959), p. 288.

[13] *Ibid.*

which they render as part of their Christian commitment. The similarity here to the New Testament pattern is evident. The members are self-consciously part of the radical reformation in their insistence on justification by faith alone and the priesthood of all believers.

The third feature is implied in the title of the movement. It is deliberately outside the institutional framework of the church. Despite the fact that the members of the Mukyokai keep the church at a distance, Brunner contends that

> it would be wrong to call them a sect or a separate church. Apart from their Bible-study groups, they have no organization whatsoever — and on principle. They have no "sacraments"; they avoid all concrete forms pertaining to the establishment of a church or sect. "The word alone will do" is their principle, taken over from Luther and out of the Bible, to which they strictly adhere. No institution, no outward and visible structure, is to hamper the free revelation and action of the Word of God and the Holy Spirit. Therefore, *Mukyokai* — Non-Church.[14]

In the light of the criticisms directed by Emil Brunner against the institutional church, it is easy to see why this Japanese movement, free as it is from so many institutional encumbrances, would appear as a movement "most promising for the future, and for all Christianity."[15]

III

The anti-institutionalists have always been with us, but they are by no means the only critics of the local church. Another group of critics, many of them sociologists, recognize that there is no way by which we can be delivered from dependence upon institutions, forms, and structures. While these can frustrate the Christian cause at times, the life of the Christian cause is unthinkable without *some* institutional embodiment with attendant forms and structures. What

[14] *Ibid.*, p. 289.
[15] *Ibid.*, p. 290.

these critics claim is quite simple: the *present* institutional forms and structures are inadequate for the Christian mission.

Tremendous changes have taken place in American life in the past few decades. All kinds of revolutions have swept across the formerly placid surface of our existence. Among all these changes there is none more important than the emergence of an urban, metropolitan society. This sweeping change was not easily recognized in its pivotal importance because it came so gradually. Its full meaning is not even yet appreciated. But one thing is surely clear: America is now an urban, metropolitan nation. The shape of America's future will be determined by what happens in and to these vast metropolitan areas. And of all the groups which like Rip Van Winkle have slept through a revolution the church stands out as one whose slumber was deepest and most prolonged. Not even now, when the issue seems so clear, is there any real assurance that the church has awakened sufficiently to set about the task of creating the new structures which may make possible mission to metropolitan America. The question about the future of American society will be answered only through the work of many groups — urban planners, architects, social scientists — and in the midst of all of them must be Christian communities which have emerged from what Gibson Winter has called "the suburban captivity of the churches."

Little time need be spent in underlining the fact that we now live in a metropolitan society. A few quick statistics can establish the fact. In 1790, five out of one hundred people lived in urban areas; by the end of the Civil War, twenty-five out of one hundred were urbanites; by the end of World War I about one-half of the population was classified as urban; and by 1950 urbanism claimed about 64 percent of the population. Now there are fourteen leading metropolitan areas and each of them has a population of at least one million. More than one-half of the total population can be found in one of these metropolitan areas.[16] Plainly, the direction of American life will be determined in these areas.

Although more and more people are living in cities, Protestantism has fled from the urban areas. The people have come, the churches have gone: this is the melancholy picture.

In the midst of this pervasive change, the local church has increasingly become remote from the actual concerns of the people and irrelevant to the decisions to be made in the public sector. The indictment of the local church, as developed by Gibson Winter, includes several counts.

The church today demonstrates, as a result of its residential base, a predominantly middle-class character. It is a one-class church, thereby denying the inclusive character of the Christian Gospel. One study, made in Pittsburgh, showed that 60 percent of the new members were gained by the churches largely through contacts with friendly members. An additional 11 percent came by contact with an organization of the church. While at first this fact may seem perfectly all right, it takes on a different aspect when compared to the composition of the usual metropolitan community. Most of the contacts made by the church members are with those of the same social and economic position. This fact renders the usual local church unable to minister effectively in the inner city because, in Winter's words,

> The central city areas . . . exhibit the two characteristics which violate the life principle of congregations of the major denominations: they have too few middle-class people; they mix middle-class people with lower-class residents.[17]

[16] Gibson Winter, *The Suburban Captivity of the Churches* (New York: Doubleday & Company, Inc., 1961), pp. 15-17. Copyright © 1961 by Gibson Winter. Reprinted by permission of Doubleday & Company, Inc.

[17] *Ibid.*, p. 70.

Not only does this middle-class composition deny the claim to inclusiveness, but it also means that the whole viewpoint of the local church becomes limited to the areas of middle-class concern.

As a direct result, the local church puts most of its emphasis upon matters of family life and the private spheres of existence. The public sector is largely forgotten. The typical local church today is made up of people who separate residence and work. The church tends increasingly to be identified with that sphere of life which touches private concerns, and the man who worships regularly in a church far removed from the place where he makes his living will soon come unconsciously to identify his faith with private concerns and view religion as a diversion from "real" affairs. This assumption is tragic.

This suburban captivity of the church is a part of the vocational crisis of the Protestant minister. The indictment of Winter is sharp and explicit:

> The Protestant minister easily becomes the number-one victim of middle-class conformity. He feels his exclusion from the producing world and missionary task principally as an enslavement to suburban children and the hypochondria which now characterizes the middle classes. He becomes a supplement to the didie service. His scholarship, preaching, teaching, and even devotion are soon drained off into the great blob of middle-class culture, a culture which subordinates the depth and meaning of religious life to the middle-class preoccupation with children.[18]

An indictment is also directed at the introverted life of the church:

> The net effect is for the church to become an end in itself — a collective symbol of the sanctity of middle-class values. When the church becomes a collective, it ceases to subordinate its identity to its reconciling task in the world. . . . The introverted church is one which puts its own survival before its mission, its own identity above its task, its internal concerns before its apostolate, its rituals before its ministry.[19]

[18] *Ibid.*, p. 79.
[19] *Ibid.*, p. 103.

The local congregation, confronting the staggering demands of mission in metropolis, must confess its inadequacy: it is too removed from the crucial areas of decision; it mirrors the brokenness of metropolis instead of showing in its life the way to healing; its denominational orientation is utterly and totally outmoded in the face of metropolitan needs. The church as the people of God will remain a necessity for Christian witness. But the local congregation must undergo radical reformation if it is to be fitted for its task.

Before this reformation can take place, basic necessities must be faced. These two necessities are based upon a recognition of two conditions: The first is that "the churches are ministering in a narrow context of accountability to the evanescent needs of an enclave — they lack a context of public accountability in the metropolis;" and the second is that they need a ministry to the expanding inner city area on "a more comprehensive base than that provided by the local congregation or parish — the Church needs a platform from which to exercise full ministry to all sectors of the metropolis."[20]

If the local congregation is to be continued at all, there is an imperative need for the development alongside it of other experimental forms and structures. These must of necessity be tentative and mobile, the sort of thing which can be called into being for a specific need and allowed to lapse without the development of vested interests which become hard to dislodge. These will be of all types, some of them with a direct connection with the church, others with very indefinite ties. Authorities in the Christian community must learn to live with structures which are not neat and precise, which will not fit readily into any sort of organizational chart. Their basic concern must not be with institutional health or growth, but rather with the Christian

[20] *Ibid.*, p. 151.

mission. The old standards of success and failure will have to be thrown quite aside, because they will not be applicable to these new structures. Conventional concepts of evangelism will have to be abandoned. Verbal evangelism may be quite out of place in the types of ventures under consideration. The idea of Christian "presence," a simple *being there,* a willingness to be silent until the moment comes to speak and to speak the word needed in that situation — no more, no less — this may be the only appropriate form of witness. Much that we formerly regarded as indispensable to Christian witness may have to be sacrificed in the name of our contemporary Christian obedience.

Beyond the need for new forms and structures, the church in metropolis has demonstrated that denominationalism is bankrupt as an instrument of metropolitan mission. This fact — I believe it can now be so described — has become very clear as the Protestant church has groped and struggled toward a viable form of mission. The search has been difficult because of our tendency to cling to the forms of the past. In a time of vast and cataclysmic changes and in the face of a situation as fraught with difficulties as urban ministry, we find the denominational form a comfort. It is, after all, *one* thing which we know. Yet this attitude invests a transient form with the finality belonging properly only to the gospel. Gibson Winter states the appalling inadequacy of denominationalism clearly: ". . . the major denominations are helpless before social differences; they cannot sustain a ministry in an area of social disorganization; yet, this is the type of area that desperately needs their ministry." In the light of this sad situation, few can dissent from the judgment that "as presently constituted, Protestantism is fighting a losing battle to minister to the metropolis."[21]

This is a melancholy picture. There is no certainty that the churches can be delivered from captivity — to the social

[21] *Ibid.,* p. 77.

stratification of American society; to the pattern of racial exclusiveness; to the separation of work and residence and hence of congregational life; to the flight to the suburbs; to the familiar ways of denominationalism; to the reduction of religion to the realm of the private and the avoidance of the public sphere. We have a church in captivity indeed!

IV

This "hard look at the church" is a venture in which the Christian believer joins with the nonbeliever. We join in this because we are convinced that mission depends upon such honest thinking. We must sketch in one more aspect. Not only are there those who are anti-institutionalist on principle; not only are there those who hold present forms and structures to be inadequate; there are also many who contend that the church is beset by a timid sort of conformity, and that it has no relevant word to speak concerning the vast public issues of our day.

This contention can be dealt with more briefly, because the failure of the church in this area is so well known. Believer and nonbeliever alike recognize this, the believer driven to penitence and the nonbeliever to scorn.

Peter Berger, a sociologist, wrote a forthright little book which caught the fancy of many because it made articulate what they dimly perceived. *The Noise of Solemn Assemblies* became an extremely popular book on college and university campuses. The basic thesis of the book is that the religious institution — the ordinary American parish — is almost totally irrelevant to the major issues of the day. Berger contends that there is a religious establishment in America that comprises most of the major denominations. The basic purpose of this establishment is the propagation and the defense of what can be called, with Will Herberg, "common faith" or, with Martin Marty, "religion-in-general." The essential mark of this faith is that it is a culture religion living upon a conviction that this is an O.K. world, that religion (if you don't define it too strictly) is "a good thing," that competition is the way of life, that religion ought to contribute to the person's peace of mind. The distinctive mark of the religious community will be its accommodation to the convictions of the society around it. The church, in short, will never utter judgments at variance with the convictions of this culture religion.

This is, according to Peter Berger, the fact of the matter. The religious establishment, however, lives on illusion, and of all such illusions one of the most persistent is that what takes place in church on Sunday bears a relation to the decisions actually made on Monday. In reality, Berger points out that

> the person listening to the minister in church is a radically different one from the person who makes economic decisions the next day. When our typical church member leaves suburbia in the morning, he leaves behind him the person that played with the children, mowed the lawn, chatted with the neighbors — and went to church. His actions now become dominated by a radically different logic — the logic of business, industry, politics, or whatever other sector of public life the individual is related to. In this second life of his the church is totally absent. What the church has said to him might conceivably have bearing on his private life. But it is quite irrelevant to his involvement in public life.[22]

Hence "the noise of solemn assemblies" may go on; but the world will not be touched by it. The church will be a harmless diversion, valid for those who happen to enjoy it.

Another sociologist, C. Wright Mills, delivered what he called "A Pagan Sermon to the Christian Clergy." It is hard-hitting and should be required reading in every Protestant seminary. Listen to these sentences:

> To understand the pivotal decisions of our times, it is not necessary to consider religious institutions or personnel or doctrine

[22] Peter L. Berger, *The Noise of Solemn Assemblies* (New York: Doubleday & Company, Inc., 1961), p. 37.

as independent forces. Neither preachers nor the religious laity matter; what they do and what they say can be readily agreed with and safely ignored. By most of those who do matter, and those who do decide, it is taken as irrelevant Sunday chatter, or it is used as an instrument of their own altogether secular purposes. . . . As a social and as a personal force, religion has become a dependent variable. . . . It does not set forth new modes of conduct and sensibility; it imitates. . . . It has become less a revitalization of the spirit in permanent tension with the world than a respectable distraction from the sourness of life.[23]

There, I submit, is preaching that hits — and hurts. The uncomfortable part of it is the truth it contains. The spectacle is too often seen of churches which are timid conformists blessing whatever is, simply because it is, never lifting even a feeble voice that might bring the church into conflict with the surrounding world of public events. This kind of church is the church of safety first — and so the church of apostasy. To too great a degree it is the modern church.

In this chapter, I have tried to let the critics speak their own mind. The picture which has emerged should make at least one thing crystal clear: the church is in need of renewal. While I have not hesitated to imply my agreement with many of the criticisms, I do not hesitate to affirm that nothing thus far said makes it possible to do away with the local church. But this must be more than an affirmation, and in the next two chapters we must see if we can state, in the light of both the seeds of disenchantment and of the criticisms of the church, a tenable case for the local church. If there is a case for the local church, then there is a meaningful role for the parish minister.

[23] C. Wright Mills, *The Causes of World War Three* (New York: Simon and Schuster, 1958), pp. 147-148.

3

THE CASE FOR
THE LOCAL CHURCH
The Scattered People of God

"The local church is dead!"

"The local church is in need of renewal."

These two statements, both of them often heard these days, are vastly different. Failure to see the difference between these two statements creates much of the confusion and no small amount of the contention in current theological thinking about the nature and mission of the church. The first statement announces a death and calls only for a proper eulogy followed by a final burial. The second statement indicates a sickness and calls for measures of cure. Our approach to the local congregation and its ministry today will be determined by which of the two statements seems to us more nearly accurate.

If the local church, as we have traditionally known it, is dead, then let us say so honestly and bury the thing with a decent sadness, remembering when the corpse lived and being duly thankful for the days of life and vigor. There is no point whatever in trying to fool ourselves; if the thing is dead, it's dead; and our wishes have no power to alter this melancholy fact.

If the local church, on the contrary, is sick and in need, not of burial, but of renewal, then let's get on with this task. This task is not helped by prophetic denunciations of the local congregation in which impatience with the church's current forms of life and witness gives judgments a quality of hyperbole which the actual situation does not warrant. Plainly, our first task is to determine whether we have on our hands an organism now functioning badly — arthritic, rheumatic, short of breath, pains in the heart, dizziness in the head — or a corpse. An organism, even a sick one, calls for one particular type of approach; a corpse calls for something quite different.

We have tried in the preceding chapter to take a hard look at the church. An attempt was made to enter into the frame of reference of those who most caustically castigate the local church. Respectfully, we listened to their denunciations, confident that most of them spoke out of a Christian passion devoted to the cause of the kingdom of God. I am convinced these Christian voices deserve to be listened to in this fashion. Nothing is to be gained by dismissing their judgments with a wave of the hand. The renewal of the church will not come about without serious and sustained attention to the areas of failure. Renewal, after all, is a most difficult task to carry through, and it can only be brought about by those who are willing to listen to what the contemporary critics of the church are saying.

For this reason we have set forth, as clearly as we know how and as often as possible in the words of the critics themselves, the catalog of futility of which they accuse the church. The voices of theologians and social scientists have thundered at us. We may well wonder after this hard look at the church if anything at all is left.

My contention can be set down quickly and briefly. The indictment of the local congregation, which can be heard everywhere, is substantially accurate. We have been shown what is wrong. The only thing I reject is the conclusion that all this wrongness adds up to the virtual death of the local church. It is my conviction, which this chapter and the following one must attempt to establish, that all of the criticism indicates much that is wrong but does not demonstrate that the local church is dead. The local congregation of believers is indispensable to the Christian enterprise. Such is my contention, and now I must try to establish it.

I

It is probably important to point out here that I am not a completely objective person in trying to do this task. Since any critics of the local church who may read these pages will quickly point out this fact, let me beat them to the punch by admitting that I am a parish minister. Not only am I a parish minister, having served now for some twenty years in this place of privilege and burden, but I make my confession that whatever measure of Christian faith I now possess I owe in significant measure to the local churches of which I have been part. This fellowship has accepted me and nurtured me, borne with me and upheld me, chastened me and encouraged me, and by its very existence reminded me continually of my Christian heritage and hence of my Christian responsibility. These factors should be set out quite clearly, since they obviously cast some degree of suspicion upon my objectivity.

But contrary to the popular adage, love is not blind. Just as a man's love for his wife leads him to see qualities in her unsuspected by others, so a man's love for the local church may lead him to see realities and beauties in it which other eyes quite completely fail to see. My love for the local church is, I hope, a critical love, the only love a Christian may properly have for any institution; but it is nevertheless love, and this should be taken into account in assessing the argument.

Listening honestly and even appreciatively to what the critics of the local congregation are saying is an indispensable discipline today. Since "the time has come for judgment to begin with the household of God" (1 Peter 4:17), we must listen. It is then our task to assess such criticism, accepting what is valid in it, modifying what may be too extreme, and rejecting what seems mistaken. This is not an easy enterprise, and all sorts of hazards beset the attempt. Because the greatest hazard is the tendency to reject all criticisms out of a misguided defensiveness, we need the difficult ability to accept the valid and reject the invalid and to do both these things out of a genuine concern that the church discover the proper form for mission in today's world.

Let me, in the light of such comments, attempt now to list in summary fashion the valid criticisms of the church. In the light of such criticisms the attempt must be made to state the case for the local church. As I see it, the following criticisms have a real measure of validity:

(1) The church suffers from morphological fundamentalism.
(2) The life of the church is too introverted.
(3) The church is too much shaped by its surrounding culture.
(4) The church carries on too many activities of dubious worth at best and positive danger at worst.
(5) The church is too much concerned with the private sphere of life and hence too little occupied in grappling with the vexing issues of the public sphere.
(6) Discipline has largely disappeared from the modern church.
(7) The church has failed to develop in its members a sense of what Christian faith involves either as belief or as a style of life.
(8) The church judges its life too much in terms of institutional success, interpreted in categories borrowed consciously or unconsciously from the surrounding culture.

There are undoubtedly other valid points in much of the current criticism of the local church. These, however, seem to me to cover the major aspects of the indictment. Within this framework of criticism honestly offered and responsibly received, I want to try to state the case for the local church.

One point must be made clear at the outset: while we have to start with the church as it is, since this is all we have, we dare not try to maintain the ecclesiastical *status quo*. This would be worse than fatal; it would be faithless. In all that is said from here on, then, we make two assumptions. The first is that renewal of the church is urgently needed. The second is that such renewal is possible, not merely by human contrivance or by dint of arduous human effort but by the power of God. Accordingly, we shall tilt a lance at those who in complacency deny the need of renewal and at those who in despair deny the possibility of renewal.

II

A rather baffling paradox confronts us at the very start. In our day we have witnessed a recovery of a genuinely biblical theology. By means of this recovery, we have been emancipated from a radically individualistic sort of thinking which imagined that the Christian life consisted in what a man does with his solitariness, as Whitehead observed, or in a flight of the "alone to the Alone," as the mystics put it. Such thinking has been shown by the current theological revival to be worlds removed from that corporate mode of thought characteristic of the Bible. Throughout the pages of the Bible man's relation to God is always a relation which he has in community with his fellows. We have found fresh meaning in such corporate concepts as the church as the people of God, the fellowship of believers, the Body of Christ, an elect nation, a royal priesthood. Inescapably we have had to face up to the fact that individualistic, solitary Christianity involves, from the biblical perspective, a contradiction in terms.

This understanding has meant a recovery of the doctrine

of the church. But the paradox in the situation is found in the manner in which many modern theologians, deeply indebted to the biblical revival, nevertheless fail to see any relevance in this doctrine of the church as a corporate reality to the church which is confronted at the local level. It is difficult to refrain from wondering just where these theologians think this corporate reality of the church does become manifest. Surely, the church is not found only in the gatherings of theologians. Nor is the church found simply in the noise of solemn ecumenical assemblies. It would seem that somewhere, if the church is a corporate body, this reality should become manifest, visible, and present. Many seem quite unwilling to acknowledge that the communal nature of the church can be found only as the church is localized.

Despite its professedly biblical rootage, a great deal of contemporary theology, in its thought about the local church, seems covertly Platonist. The theologian is committed to a view of some perfect church, existing somewhere. All actual churches are but feeble imitations of this perfect church. So far this may be all right, but a great many modern theologians — and hosts of other people as well — then proceed to believe that since the earthly reality is so imperfect they can be pardoned if they claim their membership to be in the perfect "idea" of the church. Many who are deeply concerned about the Christian faith much prefer to let their attention be fastened on that "perfect" church existing in their minds and thereby excuse themselves from responsible participation in the empirical reality of the church on the corner!

This empirical church is always to be kept under the judgment of God's will and assessed in terms of God's purpose for it. It will always, therefore, be an approximation and never a fulfillment of all that it should be. It will remain to the end of time a perplexing mixture, a human and divine institution. And always our devotion to the existing church will have in it something of the mood of the churchman who said the church was like Noah's Ark — if it were not for the storm outside you could never stand the smell inside!

III

The church as the scattered people of God is one of the emphases of the newer currents of theology. In the light of what this emphasis says about the church, let us see whether or not it makes the local church superfluous. The basic thrust of this point of view begins with the conviction that the past form of Christian witness has been sadly deficient because that witness has been too narrowly defined as a matter of bringing some people, now caught out in the "world" into the life of the church. According to this older concept the world is widely regarded as the enemy of the spirit, and redemption is found by being taken out of the world into the realm of the church. In line with this type of thinking, the good Christian can be identified by certain quick, rule-of-thumb tests. A good Christian is one who gives himself or herself with devotion to the life of the church. Service on boards and committees, teaching in the church school, and providing leadership for the multifarious activities of the modern church are some of the criteria. If every evening of such a person's time is taken by the church, there is a tendency to think that he is a dedicated Christian.

Consistent with this approach the ideal type of church is characterized by a bustle of activity, most of which centers within the church building. Seven days and nights a week there is "something going on in the building." Activities are planned for all persons from tots hardly able to walk to the elderly just able to get about. Some of these activities, if critically examined, have almost no relation to the basic task of the church. But this is rarely the criterion.

The important matter is to get people, no matter by what means, within the confines of the church building. By some mysterious process, the building itself is supposed to contribute to their growth in the things of the spirit. To face the searching question — "How much of all this activity could be tossed out tomorrow without any real loss to the important work of the church as the people of God" — is to be made acutely uncomfortable. We are forced to face up to the possibility that our busyness may be a hiding place from the real summons of God who makes himself known in the tangled realities of daily existence.

Impatience with this kind of churchiness has led to the contemporary emphasis upon the church as the scattered people of God. If the Christian faith is really to touch life with any sort of impact, making itself felt where the crucial decisions are being made, the faith must be taken beyond the church building. Many structures of life need to be penetrated by Christian forces. The political life needs Christian men and women who as Christians will take their place in the life of political parties. The world of business organization needs the witness of Christian persons. The world of union labor needs to be informed by the concerns of Christian faith. So the list could go on, but the point surely is plain: there is a world in which decisive and life-shaping decisions are being made every day. The Christian faith can never have any influence upon the shape and structure of such decisions unless and until Christian people get out of the church's hectic life and into the world of everyday existence. Thus will the church be scattered abroad throughout all the levels and structures of society.

This approach has come to many in the modern church like a breath of fresh spring air. It has seemed to be the answer to the musty, introverted life of the church. This concept opens up the rather thrilling possibility that our faith may begin to make itself felt in connection with the life-and-death issues of this day and age. Under the banner of the church as the scattered people of God, hosts of the new generation of ministers have turned away from the life of the institutional church at the corner of Main and First Streets to what seems to be the far more thrilling matter of bearing witness in the social movements of our day, in the various forms of chaplaincy, or in the venture of teaching. Many others have taken this emphasis as a charter whereby their Christian vocation can be more responsibly exercised outside the pastoral ministry than would have ever been possible within it.

Because I believe so deeply in the validity of the concept of the church as the scattered people of God, I want to stress the importance of the local church and hence the worthwhileness of the pastoral ministry. Such a concept makes the church and the pastoral ministry not less important but more vital than ever before. More than that, this whole concept, properly understood and rightly implemented in the church and in the determination of our priorities in the pastoral ministry, can be a liberating experience, helping us to get back to the tasks which are really vital and enabling us to say a firm farewell to a lot of the ridiculous antics through which we are now expected to go in the local church.

IV

However, the whole thrust of the church in the world idea loses its relevance and its dynamic if it is not seen to be the *church* in the midst of society. We do not simply scatter people; we scatter the *people of God*. As it is currently employed, the concept of the scattered church gives too little consideration to the type of person who is thus to be the church in his or her place in the world. Failure to realize the difficulty of witness in the world leads us to underestimate the degree to which the contemporary layman must be prepared for this kind of task.

The failure to understand either the nature of the world in which he witnesses or the man who does the witnessing explains the weakness of our Christian impact and our failure to recognize the role of the local church. The modern layman is woefully unprepared to carry on the task which he has been assigned in the current emphasis upon the scattered church. He is not prepared because he does not know with any clarity what he believes, nor does he understand with any depth how his faith touches his daily existence. He may be good, earnest, honest, sincere, as many laymen unquestionably are, but all too often he does not have a really adequate understanding of the faith he professes.

This judgment is in part subjective and in part objective. It is based upon one man's experience in dealing for over twenty years with laymen. Let it be admitted that any judgment that laymen are defective in their grasp of Christian faith and its implications for life is a judgment upon myself as a minister. Their failure is my failure, and I dare not seek to place the onus of responsibility solely upon the laymen. The failure is the failure of the local church, and at this point we must acknowledge the fact of our failure and seek to overcome it.

Whatever the proper location of responsibility for this situation, the melancholy fact remains. The vast majority of the lay people of the modern church do not really understand what the Christian faith is all about. Because they do not know what the faith really is, they are quite unprepared to bear witness to that faith in the world where perplexing decisions must be faced daily. They do not really see how faith has any meaning for daily life. For such a long time they have viewed their Christian life as something which had to do with "church" that they cannot even begin to see how their Christian faith has any meaning for their economic, racial, and political decisions. Much of modern Christian strategy, which sounds perfectly wonderful in ecumenical conclaves, will founder on the rocks of practical reality because our strategy concerning the scattered people of God presupposes a people which does not yet exist, a laity which is articulate about the Christian faith and sophisticated in understanding the relation of the faith to concrete decisions.

Perhaps it is a measure of my own inadequacy, but I have never had a laity like that. Nor have I ever seen such laity in other local churches. Other men in the pastoral ministry have also shared their impressions that the situation is almost desperate, and that the laymen they know are seriously adrift when it comes to any real understanding of faith and its implications.

This subjective judgment is strengthened whenever the basic issues of Christian belief are faced with a group of lay people in the church. Along with a widespread desire to know faith at a more adequate level, there is an uneasiness when the discussion begins to touch the fundamental matters of belief. This feeling is very hard to define and describe. People seem to be afraid lest the precious little faith they possess will be dissipated if they begin to look at it candidly and to think about it deeply. They will nibble around the edges of vast questions but scurry away to safer ground when the discussion begins to focus on deeper issues.

These judgments, however, are subjective, the reactions of one pastor which may or may not be supported by other pastors. A number of observers, who are not pastors, have confirmed these impressions. Dorothy Sayers, for example, commented on the laymen in England: ". . . the more or less instructed churchgoers . . . are about as well equipped to do battle on fundamentals against a Marxian atheist or a Wellsian agnostic as a boy with a pea-shooter facing a fanfire or machine-guns."[1]

[1] Dorothy Sayers, *Creed or Chaos?* (New York: Harcourt, Brace, & World, Inc., 1949), p. 29.

The situation in all its seriousness is by no means confined to England. An American, out of long experience in teaching and close contact with the people of the churches, wrote in *The Christianity of Main Street:*

> This Christianity of Main Street is a peculiar Christianity. It is a Christianity without doctrinal foundations, or one resting on such shallow foundations as to endanger the superstructure. . . . It is now on its own and sees little need of the doctrinal framework of belief out of which it once emerged.[2]

Many pastors will recognize the accuracy of the foregoing as a description of the Christianity found in any number of churches along many main streets in America.

Without a desire to labor the obvious, I want to cite two more bits of evidence, because this point is crucial to the case I want to try to establish: the conviction that the layman, as he is at present, is not equipped to do what the avant garde theologians are urging upon him and that he can be prepared for his task only by a deeper experience of the Christian community and its faith in the life and witness of the local church. Roy Fairchild and John Charles Wynn undertook a survey, on behalf of the United Presbyterian Church, of the relationship of families to the church. They studied in depth a good many families. It is important to understand that their study as it actually worked out involved them in a consideration of people who were even more active in the church than Fairchild and Wynn really wanted; that is, they did not have an opportunity to study the inactive or peripheral members. This is their conclusion:

> We might therefore have expected an unusually enlightened response to the Christian faith and an articulateness about the Reformed heritage in theology. But this we did not find. They seldom displayed any sure grasp of the distinctive elements inherent in Protestant Christianity. It was not uncommon for them to reveal

[2] T. O. Wedel, *The Christianity of Main Street* (New York: The Macmillan Company, 1950), pp. 2-3.

some embarrassment about any religious tenet or practice that made them seem or feel different from their neighbors.[3]

The final witness I want to call deals with the religious beliefs of youth. Murray G. Ross studied the religious beliefs of 1,935 young people by means of a questionnaire and by intensive interviews with one hundred other young people. The foreword to the book incorporating the results of the research was written by the distinguished psychologist, Gordon W. Allport, who concludes:

> For the majority of youth religion in large part seems like a remote if pleasant memory. What it teaches is unclear and its bearing on present activities is dim. To borrow Renan's phrases, its nostalgic quality is like the perfume of an empty vase.[4]

The evidence, then, is before us, and there is little reason to believe that any significant changes have been made to alter this picture of the layman which casts considerable doubt upon his ability to be a part of the church in the world. He may be in the world, but can this layman really be the church in the world? The answer suggested by the analysis thus far is a definite No.

V

An additional factor must be taken into account in the consideration of the concept of the scattered church. This factor is the nature of the world into which lay people are sent. We tend greatly to underestimate the power of that world to shape people in terms of its own reality and its tendency not only to alter but in many instances completely to smash the belief of lay people. If the church, in its justifiable concern about dispersing Christian witness in the

[3] Roy W. Fairchild and John Charles Wynn, *Families in the Church: A Protestant Survey* (New York: Association Press, 1961), pp. 167-168.

[4] Murray G. Ross, *Religious Beliefs of Youth* (New York: Association Press, 1950), p. vii.

world, fails to understand the real nature of the world, it will have sent people into the world quite unprepared to deal with its sobering realities.

We can appreciate something of the threat involved in this kind of venture if we look in some detail at the story of one of the creative ventures in scattering the church in the world. The experiment, conducted by the Roman Catholic Church in France, with the so-called priest-workers has a fascination for anyone interested in responsible Christian witness, and it holds some important lessons for those who wish to develop a relevant type of Christian action.

The beginning of the experiment was stimulated by a little book, prepared at the request of Cardinal Suhard, Archbishop of Paris, which explored the relationship between the church and the working classes in France. The report became a sensation, especially influencing young priests. Entitled *France, Pagan?*, the book emphasized how foolish it was for the priests to go on in the traditional way

> saying Mass in their cold and empty churches for a few middle-aged spinsters and reluctant altar boys, when the vast majority of Frenchmen, and especially the industrial workers, had lost contact with the Church altogether and could only be approached in a "missionary" spirit. . . . with a technique adapted to their special circumstances.[5]

The special technique was developed out of the experience of the days of World War II, when young priests went with the workers from France conscripted into German industry. They lived with the workers as workers themselves. This approach was adopted as the technique of the "Mission de Paris," to be followed shortly by similar missions in Lyons and Marseilles.

The young men who went into the venture were priests.

[5] *Priest and Worker: The Autobiography of Henri Perrin* (New York: Holt, Rinehart and Winston, Inc., 1964). The quotation is from the Introduction, "The Drama of the Priest-Workers," by Bernard Wall, p. 5.

There was a sense of the danger involved in this venture, and it was therefore recognized that great care had to be exercised in the selection of the men who would undertake this particular mission. In a report of July, 1950, the care exercised in selection was made very plain:

> In effect, the requirements are for priests who are obviously well-balanced physically, intellectually and morally; who possess a sound culture in philosophy and theology; and lastly who have a fair experience of pastoral work.
>
> Furthermore, we systematically eliminate those who are attracted by a taste for novelty.
>
> We turn down visionaries, men who are carried away by a kind of working-class romanticism, but are really narrow-minded. The sort who imagine it is only necessary to be a worker in order to be good, and who think only of the salvation of the working-class, to the exclusion of the other classes.
>
> We are specially careful to avoid taking in unstable characters or blunderers. . . .
>
> For preference, priests are chosen who come from parochial work. Some of them have been performing it for five, eight, eleven or even eighteen years. Their ages range from twenty-eight to fifty-eight, and the average is about thirty-five.
>
> All have followed the usual university studies in France. Some have studied at the Universities of Rome, Paris or Strasbourg. The priests of the Mission to Paris include one Doctor, one Master and one Bachelor of Theology and two Masters in Canon Law.[6]

This report makes very clear that those who were selected as members of this apostolate were priests who were as well equipped as men could be to face the challenges which would surely confront them. Cardinal Suhard expressed the task of the priest-workers in these words:

> It is therefore important that priests become witnesses (temoins) again, not so much to convince, as to be a sign. . . . That is, to live in such a way that life is meaningless if God does not exist: to bear witness less thorough [sic, through] outward changes of the forms of life than by their [the worker-priests'] firm will *to enter*

[6] *The Worker-Priests: A Collective Documentation*, John Petrie, trans. (New York: The Macmillan Company and London: Routledge & Kegan Paul, 1956), p. 121.

*a real community of destiny with the disinherited masses. . . . * For them the work is neither a pretense nor an opportunity to propagandize, but rather the natural assumption by the priest of his place among the people where he had been almost a stranger.[7]

The priest-worker was to live with the proletarian masses, to work side by side with them, to share their life totally and completely, including their uncertainty and their anxiety. In short, the priest-workers, except for the fact that they were celibate and said Mass in their rooms, were very much in the same situation as the Protestant laymen.

In the light of this similarity the story of the priest-workers becomes very important for our consideration. The actual details of what happened are very complex and no quick, neat generalization can be either complete or fair. The experiment from the outset was looked upon with suspicion by some of the conservative groups in the Roman Catholic Church in France. Rightist elements in French society were also skeptical. The fears of the conservative elements were not so important because they reflected the typical bourgeois apprehensiveness about any contact with the working classes.

There was, however, a deeper and more honorable fear at work. The largest trade union in France was clearly Communist-controlled. Yet the priest-workers, if they sought truly to be part of the working-class world, could not stand aloof from that group. The membership of the priest-workers in the union, and especially their activities in the leadership of unions, created a fear in the minds of their ecclesiastical superiors that they were becoming too deeply influenced by Marxist thought, especially the idea of the class struggle. Consequently, for a variety of reasons, some good, some bad, the experiment was halted and the priests were told to return to their parish duties.

[7] Quoted by Friedrich Heer, "The Priest-Workers in France: Origin and Backgrounds," *Cross Currents*, Vol. 4 (1953-54), p. 265.

However, in October of 1965, the effort was renewed with certain changes that underscore not only the problems encountered in this Roman Catholic experience, but also the problems facing the Protestant layman who is called to be a part of the church in the world. The name was changed from priest-worker to working-priest, thus emphasizing the fact that those involved in the apostolate were to be first of all priests and then workers. They were to avoid all participation in political movements, and while permitted to join labor unions, could not hold office in such organizations. They were to receive more careful training than ever before — a fact of considerable importance in light of the average Protestant layman's lack of special training to be a Christian witness. Most significant of all, they were not permitted to live alone. "They may live in the workers' quarters, but with other priests." [8]

If it became necessary to develop such safeguards to protect men as deeply and as well-trained as are members of the Roman Catholic priesthood against the influence of the working world, how much of a witness can be expected from Protestant laymen who are so pathetically unequipped for the struggle?

The need for training the laity for "the equipment of the saints, for the work of ministry" (Ephesians 4:12 RSV) is clearer than ever before. The imperative necessity of this pastoral ministry brings us once again to a recognition of the importance, worth, and strategic centrality of the pastoral office.

The Protestant layman has been sent out into the world. There we have said to him, in effect, "You are the church at that spot. You are to be in the world as a Christian, taking your faith with utter seriousness and bearing witness to it in the decisions of your daily existence."

This thrilling venture requires men who are very care-

[8] John Cogley, "They Are Priests and Workers, Both," *The New York Times Magazine,* December 26, 1965, pp. 6, 33-36.

fully trained. Perhaps in our zeal to get the Christian faith outside the walls of the church building and into the common life, we have placed upon the Protestant layman a burden he is not yet able to bear. We may well have expected to scatter the church through the world before we have made sure that the church really exists. We have scattered men and women in the world while neglecting the responsibility which rests upon the church to arm and train these witnesses for their demanding task in the world.

The exciting concept of the scattered church, then, may become the basis for a new estimate of the centrality of the local church although not the local church as it now is known. Plainly reform and renewal are urgently required if the local church is to fulfill its basic task of preparing men and women to be the church in the world. We may have to come to appreciate anew and afresh the reality of faith as a way of life and as a basis of the fellowship of people in God, before we are really ready to be effective as the church in the world. Perhaps, in summary, we must gather the scattered people of God for worship, teaching, and fellowship until the life of the community of faith becomes so much a part of them that they can withstand the subtle pressures of the world. Perhaps we must still say that local churches, sadly deficient though they may be, remain the indispensable training centers for the Christian witness in our day. If the laity do not find their training within the local church, where are they to gain it? And until a clearer alternative emerges out of the thunder of denunciations, the local church must continue as the manifestation in a particular time and place of the universal church.

The laymen, then, must be scattered in the world, for only in this fashion can the Christian faith make an impact upon the world of daily existence. But if the laymen are going to do this effectively, they must also be gathered.

4

THE CASE FOR
THE LOCAL CHURCH
The Gathered People of God

A tremendous burden has been placed upon the layman. He is summoned to be the church at a particular spot in the world. It is not surprising if he finds this vocation a demanding one, and as a result yearns for some secure haven where bearing witness is not fraught with such complex difficulties. The previous chapter has attempted to focus attention upon this layman and to show the importance of his place in the world. It was suggested that we can safely and effectively "scatter" the Christian laymen only after we have carefully "gathered" them into the life of the local church.

We do not have to make a choice between the church gathered and the church scattered. Both emphases are needed, and no view is complete which forces a choice between these two emphases. While accepting the validity of the concept of the scattered church, we have also said, however, that the layman of today is not really ready for this kind of radical witness. He needs to be gathered into the life of the local church, letting that be the place where he secures sustaining fellowship, and expresses the need of his humanity to worship and adore God. Without this kind of participation in the community of faith, the modern layman will not make much headway in the task of bearing witness in the vexing and demanding spheres of the common life.

The essential validity of the insight that the church is a servant community is not at issue; this claim is accepted, not grudgingly but gladly, and everything which takes place when the church is gathered should have meaning for the time when the church is again scattered to share in God's purpose for the world. In contrast, the old idea, by which many in the present generation of men in the pastoral ministry were trained, would be summarized in this fashion: out of the world, into the church. Much of the energy of the church was devoted to bringing about this result. Out of this came the emphasis upon mass evangelism and the importance attached to the internal life of the local church. When people had been brought into the life of the local church, the task was considered virtually completed. All that was then required was to keep those brought in active and busy and, hopefully, growing in Christ. Hence many men found their basic ideas of their vocational responsibility focusing around this approach. To bring people out of the world and into the church and then to give them things to do which would keep them active in the life of the church: such was the conventional idea of ministerial responsibility.

The new concept is quite different. It can be summarized in this fashion: out of the church, into the world. It is still very important to bring people into the church, but this is not the culmination of the task. People are brought in to prepare them to go out again. The focus now falls upon their life when they are outside the walls of the church. What is done in the church is significant only as it prepares people for witness in the world. The task of the local church is to view its own life as a means by which the laity are prepared to be the church in the world. But the difficulty which many pastors find with this sort of approach is found in the fact that it is so new, so different from what they thought they were supposed to be doing. It is akin to a Copernican revolution, and a revolution is never easy to undergo, especially when in the process it calls into question all the easy assumptions by which life had been guided from day to day. This is precisely what has happened to many men in the pastoral ministry today. They are in a new realm where there are no charts or maps to guide them. About all they know is that they are summoned to a new form of Christian witness and that the determination of its exact structure is going to be a long and difficult task.

In this situation, any precise delineation of the shape of the local church for its new mission can hardly be expected. Yet it is important to try to give some idea of what the life of the gathered people of God would be like. Everything in this area must be offered very tentatively; what will be set down here should be viewed as gropings, timid approaches to a very difficult problem.

The task in this area is so difficult because new emphases must be added to existing programs. Part of the problem of renewal of an institution is that the heavy hand of the past and its hallowed procedures is always present. The ways of the fathers can be an inspiration to the sons; they can also be a positive hindrance to the effectiveness of the witness of the sons. Every age makes fresh demands upon the church, and hence each generation must try to change and adapt its procedures to make sure that faithfulness in witness is achieved. It would, of course, be a great deal easier if we could wipe the slate entirely clean and start quite fresh. This can never be done. What is required, therefore, is insight to see the legitimate claims of the new emphases; and patience to work with the church as it is, in such a fashion that the local church is renewed in its life and reformed in its procedures.

I

With this qualification let me now try to indicate what the life of the gathered church might be like. Here we shall attempt to conserve the valid emphases of the local church as it is and to change whatever is not making a significant contribution to the effective witness of the scattered people of God.

The church is no less enticed by the novel than any other institution. The fear of "the same old thing" is present at all times in the church. It is quite wrong to act as though the only danger the church faces is that of a firm traditionalism. The danger represented by the attraction of the new and novel is no less real. What is merely fashionable can be just as attractive as the merely traditional. To embrace the latest fad is no guarantee of being faithful.

This is especially the case when we come to consider the matter of the church's own essential being. The church is, after all, a community with roots stretching far back into the past. For centuries the church has lived by certain actions which are linked with the church's essential being. If these actions were removed, anything that could be defined as "church" would also be likely to disappear. This is not to enter into any argument about the worth of these actions; it is only to recognize, for the moment, that these actions are what give the church its life.

One basic action is the provision for and the conduct of common worship. For generations this has been the church's distinctive emphasis. While the church has done many other things in addition to this, this action has identified the church as a distinctive community. Many functions once carried on by the church have in the course of time been taken over by other agencies in the community. The conduct of public worship remains, however, the distinctive task of the gathered church.

This action is not to be retained by the church simply

because it is the one function not likely to be taken over by other agencies. The action is to be retained by the church because it is the church's own life. Apart from this act the church has no life. The church is constituted, indeed, by the hearing of the Word and the celebration of the sacraments. Nothing in the years since Calvin uttered this definition of the church has really altered the situation.

It is difficult, however, to hold to this basic task with real fidelity. Worship may very easily be crowded out of the church's life until the provision for and conduct of public worship becomes a function to be carried through in a perfunctory manner and with as little drain on resources as can be decently permitted. Every era of the church's history can provide an example of the way in which worship, far from being the central and life-constituting activity of the church, has become a peripheral activity. Subject as the church has always been to fads of one kind or another, there have been those who claimed that the social gospel would save the world by heroic Christian social action; the ardent advocates of Christian education who proposed to accomplish the Christian task by the careful development of the mind; the ecumenical enthusiasts who imagined that unity would be a guarantee of mission instead of *vice versa;* and the liturgical experts who seemed to be more intent on creating a certain "feeling" in people than in the adoration of God. Within the past few generations, all these enthusiasms have captured the church. Quite frequently in the process the church as a worshiping community has been lost.

We are once more in such a period. It is essential to make a distinction here between two moods. One is, I believe, always to be welcomed because it is a constant necessity in the church. The other is unfortunate, because it is a denial rather than a realization of the church's distinctive task.

The proper mood is a feeling of impatience with the

public worship of the church. Like every activity carried on by the church, the worship service needs constantly to be kept under the judgment of the concerned Christian conscience. The feeling of many today that public worship is dead and barren, dry and lifeless, has a measure of real validity. Worship can be an affair of liturgical correctness quite unrelated to life. Or worship can be related to life but so sloppy that it carries no sense of the holy and the transcendent. In either case, worship must be judged and found deficient. No forms, however hallowed by age, can be kept sacrosanct; they are forms only, and the content must be supplied by the grappling of men with the issues of life and the reality of faith in every age.

The improper mood is one which lets impatience with the inadequacy of the church's public worship produce a flippant dismissal of worship itself. This can easily be understood. So often the worship of the church leaves much to be desired: preaching which stays safely on the surface, prayers which never break open men's hearts to the Divine, sacraments which treat vast matters with perfunctory diffidence, music which bounces along intent on giving the people what they can enjoy. Such worship, if it can be called that, deserves to be judged and needs desperately to be transformed. But this does not mean that we can then dismiss worship itself. This faulty conclusion sometimes emerges from correct analyses.

The present situation is once again one in which the venture of public worship is often treated with indifference. Sometimes public worship seems to be inane because in the concept of the church as the scattered people of God the emphasis is upon social action. The great cry of our day is that the church must be where the great issues are being decided. It is quite plain that in the local church, gathered for public worship, no great issue is being decided. The whole activity, in a day of vast public issues of life-and-death, seems at best innocuous time-wasting.

There is an interesting illustration of this feeling about worship in connection with the work of the East Harlem Protestant Parish. This venture, begun by some young graduates of Union Theological Seminary, has excited the interest and won the admiration of many. Both the interest and the admiration are abundantly deserved. The East Harlem Protestant Parish has grappled with the meaning of Christian witness in a crowded city slum. It has sought to find a form of church life which would give meaning and purpose to existence in East Harlem. Naturally, there have been mistakes and a tendency to imagine that the church outside the East Harlem Protestant Parish is dead and that its only hope is to remold itself upon the pioneering outlines of the East Harlem model. This certitude is quite natural and to be expected and should certainly not diminish our admiration of the courage or the vision of the ministry of East Harlem.

An interesting point, however, is the reaction to the East Harlem Protestant Parish of a layman who was involved for a time in its life. As a young lawyer William Stringfellow went to East Harlem and became associated with the parish. What he found disturbed him, for he felt that the young ministers had left out of their concern the basic matter of the church's real life. William Stringfellow writes:

> The Church is much tempted by conformity to the world, by accommodating the message and mission to the particular society in which the Church happens to be, . . . This temptation beguiled the group ministry of the East Harlem Protestant Parish. They plunged into all sorts of social work and social action. . . . But they neglected and postponed the proclamation and celebration of the Gospel in East Harlem. In the congregations of the parish, the Bible was closed; in the group ministry there was even scorn for the Bible as a means through which the Word of God is communicated in contemporary society. The liturgical life of the congregations grew erratic and fortuitous, depending upon the personality and whim, even, of the minister presiding at the time.[1]

[1] William Stringfellow, *My People Is the Enemy* (New York: Holt, Rinehart & Winston, Inc., 1964), pp. 88-89.

After about fifteen months William Stringfellow left the parish. He felt that the East Harlem Protestant Parish, by its neglect of the Bible at that time, by its lack of concern for liturgy, by its failure to achieve effective lay participation in parish decisions, was demonstrating not the model of the church needed in our day but a kind of romanticism. Here is a case of a layman calling the church to a realization that its purpose was not to conform to its setting whether in suburbia or slum, but to call men to the venture of adoration of God in common worship. Only as the church did this, whether it met with great popular rejoicing or not, would the church really fulfill its proper role, which is the justification for its life in the world.

The church in the slums or in suburbia finds it difficult to keep its attention fixed upon the centrality of public worship. Yet worship is what the layman needs most desperately. If he is to bear his witness effectively in the world, he needs to live by the principle of withdrawal and return. While we have put our emphasis today upon the return, upon the life in the world, we dare not overlook the necessity for him to have a respite from this witness during which he recovers the sense of the presence of God so easily lost in the welter of the world's distractions. It would be utter folly to imagine that such an emphasis upon worship would win the church great plaudits from the people or seem very exciting. But the church is a community of adoration, finding its very reason for existence in its praise of God and its celebration of God's graciousness toward man. Without this dimension, the church is simply one more institution, little different from a hundred others, and the layman, so desperately in need of the perspective and refreshment of public worship, will find his soul stifled and God dim and unreal.

Daniel Jenkins has expressed clearly the fundamental note of the life of the gathered people of God. He points out that the first task of the church is to

*insist on the primacy and indispensability of the characteristic
church actions,* through which the Church maintains decisive contact with the sources of its own distinctive life. Nothing must be
allowed to detract from the centrality in the Church's life of faithful preaching, the celebration of the sacraments, the public reading
of the Scriptures and the prayers, and from the closely-knit community life in church order which maintains and is sustained by
these.[2]

To all who would persuade the church to follow enticing
bypaths, the church must say: "O come, let us worship. . . ."

Only this experience of worship in which God becomes
real can equip the layman for his witness. Failure to keep
worship in a central place may result only from an inability
to realize the extent to which the world seems God-forsaken.
Cast out in such a world, the layman may very readily
begin to feel that God is unreal, faith an illusion, and the
Christian venture a foolish dream. Public worship then
breaks into the midst of such doubt as a life-giving affirmation of the reality, the glory, and above all, the love of
God. Having withdrawn for a few moments, the layman is
prepared to go back to the world, sure that what he has
just professed in his worship is true also in his world.

But this result can only come about if the church's worship is unashamedly intent upon the glory of God. If the
layman, whom we have been trying to keep central in our
thought in these pages, is going to carry on a ministry in
the world, he must be prepared by being given a sense
of the reality of the presence of God in the gathered worship of the local congregation. Without this periodic renewal of his deepest convictions, without this setting of his
life and witness in the proper perspective of a relation to
God as the holy and transcendent source of all being, the
layman is almost inevitably going to be overcome by the
denials of a world which does not know God in this way.

[2] Daniel Jenkins, *Beyond Religion* (Philadelphia: The Westminster
Press, 1962), p. 108. Copyright © 1962, W. L. Jenkins. Used by
permission.

In his book *How the Church Can Minister to the World Without Losing Itself,* Langdon Gilkey has dealt in helpful fashion with exactly this problem. He, too, accepts the validity of the contention that the church must be the servant community, and that Christians are therefore called to show that servanthood in responsible living in the affairs of daily life. But he sees, more clearly and responsibly than many writers in this field, that this very calling makes the gathered life of worship, of attendance upon Word and Sacrament, more vitally important than ever before. He provides an apt illustration which makes the point we have been endeavoring to stress in this and the preceding chapter. When he was a member of the faculty at Vassar College, he was sometimes asked to take charge of the worship of the local Friends Meeting. He once asked the man in charge of the meeting why they no longer conducted the worship in the usual manner of Friends, depending upon no minister in a formal sense and having no sermon in the usual meaning of the word. The reply to Gilkey is instructive:

> "I was raised a Quaker in a Quaker family, and grew up surrounded by a Quaker community — and the Inner Light spoke to all of us at the meetings we had together. But when we moved here to Poughkeepsie, and I began to sell stocks and bonds, all I could think of in that silence was the Dow-Jones stock averages — and so we wanted to have people who didn't think only of the market all week long to talk to us about religion."

Dr. Gilkey adds the comment:

> One could put his — and our — problem this way: when the whole of a man's life is suffused with contact with the divine, in daily Bible reading, the requirements of a strict communal ethic, and constant habits of prayer, then through the total character of his life his subjectivity is saturated with the dimension of the holy, and he can go into a bare room, sit in silence, and religious and ethical wisdom wells up inside him. But the man whose daily life is immersed in secular, cultural, and business affairs, who seldom reads the Bible, and whose life of personal prayer is at

best feeble, erratic, and unsure — when *he* goes to that bare room, divested of all religious symbols and all objective media for the holy, there is no holy *anywhere* for him to experience, and his mind is filled, and naturally so, with the stuff of his life, Dow-Jones stock averages.[3]

This situation is precisely that in which most Protestant laymen, whatever may be their church affiliation, now find themselves. The world of daily life can so completely fill their minds that the realities of faith are not so much explicitly denied as choked out. Any authentic Christian faith is concerned with what a man is as well as with what he does. As Gilkey puts it,

Thus "religion," taken as referring to that inner relation of repentance, trust, and obedience to God, is not antithetical to, but the foundation of, "true worldliness" in the sense of acts of mercy and love to the world around. . . . This concern with God, with His claim on us, with His judgment of us and His freeing love and mercy toward us, must remain the nuclear center of the church's life in order to make possible the community of love and the acts of reconciliation it offers to the world.[4]

It must once again be emphasized that we are not saying that the worship of the gathered church is now all that it should be. Plainly, a great deal needs to be done, especially at the point of making sure that worship is not an activity totally isolated from daily life. Worship must always have a window that opens out upon that world in which the layman must carry on his witness. Worship should make clear that the final denial of the Lordship of Christ is to confine him to the pious exercises of Sunday morning. Worship, in short, can no longer be permitted to deal only with the private sphere; it must constantly keep in mind and be relevant to the public sphere. However, that worship which

[3] Langdon Gilkey, *How the Church Can Minister to the World Without Losing Itself* (New York: Harper & Row, Publishers, Inc., 1964), p. 111.
[4] *Ibid.*, p. 27.

is confined to the world will finally fail to equip the layman properly to serve God or to love his neighbor in that world. For it is the reality of God which equips the layman for this task; and worship can communicate the reality of God only when it is not completely identified with the world. What this means is that worship, like every activity in which the Christian takes part, is best described as being in a state of tension, in this case between involvement and withdrawal. Without involvement in the affairs of the world the withdrawal is irresponsible; without withdrawal the involvement is likely to be ineffective.

The gathered community, whatever else it may be, must be a community of worship and adoration. Only the view of God high and lifted up will strengthen resolve, clarify purposes, and purge unrighteousness.

II

The gathered community will have other marks of its common life. In addition to the life of worship, the gathered church must be an instrument of education, of training, and of instruction. The plight of today's layman, set out in the midst of a world torn apart by various ideologies, has been dealt with in foregoing pages. This layman and his witness in the world must be kept constantly in our minds as we think of the ways in which the life of the gathered community can be helpful to him.

The truth seems clear and inescapable that the church has not in the past fulfilled its teaching task with any adequacy at all. There are many reasons for this. The failure roots partly in a one-sided emphasis upon an emotional conversion experience and the conclusion that once he had this experience the new Christian could be left pretty much to his own devices. A strong strain of anti-intellectualism runs through most of the Protestant churches. Learning has always been looked upon with a certain suspicion. Out of this atmosphere, quite understandably, there has emerged the lack of concern for the teaching task of the church.

A second source of this lack of educational concern has been a fear of the divisive nature of doctrinal teaching. There has been an unconscious prejudice against whatever would make the Christian approach to life different from that of the surrounding culture. Hence a very popular reception is always given to any interpretation of Christianity as just an adjunct to the nation's Way of Life. If this interpretation is true, then we need not worry that our profession of Christian faith will in any way set us against our neighbors. As long as we avoid whatever is distinctive, we shall not create division. We shall then be adherents of a sort of homogenized outlook, blending all distinctiveness in a mild mixture of culture-faith.

Precisely this sort of amalgamation cannot be done if the task of teaching the authentic Christian faith to the laity is taken seriously. For this faith is at the very least a clear, specific, definite way of looking at life and destiny. It is far more than a culture religion; it is an outlook which judges all cultures. To teach this kind of faith and not some pallid substitute is to confront the peril of division.

A third reason for the church's abandonment of the task of training the laity is that we have been so ignorant of theology that we have not really known how to teach it. What this means is that we have put so much emphasis upon Christianity as a way of life, a matter of ethical endeavor, that we have not come to grips with the fact that Christianity is also a way of thinking. Perhaps there is even a connection between our theological ignorance and our ethical ineffectiveness. Perhaps we shall know as Christians what to *do* only when we have determined who and whose we are — and these are questions of theology.

This list of reasons is, of course, not exhaustive, and is not intended to be. Against the background of these reasons we need to take a fresh look at the church's educational task. This task centers in the training of the laity for mission in the world.

The typical church of today thinks of its educational task largely in the traditional pattern of the Sunday school for children and young people. Whatever adult education is done is carried on in a perfunctory manner. Often it is only a form of parent-sitting while the church tries to do something with the children who are potentially open to the impact of the gospel. This conception of the church's educational task must be completely cast aside if the church is to face up to its responsibility of preparing the laity for mission.

The focus of primary educational concern, on this proposed basis, will be the adults. The children will, of course, continue to be trained and educated in the Christian faith, and hopefully in a far better fashion than in the past. But the church, and especially the minister, must undergo a revolution in outlook so that the adults will become the primary claimants upon the educational insight and energy of church and minister.

We cannot really do more than touch the surface of the changes which are urgently needed in this area. To sketch out a full-range educational program for the church intent upon mission in the world is beyond the scope of this book. However, some hints of the shape such an educational program might take will be suggested.

The basic premise with which we begin is this: The present situation reveals a church and a laity who know little of the foundations of Christian faith and hence any renewal must begin by giving the laity some rootage in the basic doctrines of the Christian faith. Without this basis of renewal, nothing creative can take place in the modern church.

If this sort of approach is to be utilized, we shall have to be ready to experiment with a variety of approaches. The conventional Sunday morning class will not be sufficient.

Because the whole Sunday school movement is a recent innovation, we are not terribly radical if we suggest that some changes in its format are long overdue. With the increasing leisure time available, the church has an opportunity to involve the laity in a quest for deeper roots of Christian belief and action. Evening meetings in homes, breakfasts for men on the way to work, coffees for housewives — all these are means which are being grasped by the church to involve members in the search for authentic faith.

These experiments, all of them involving small groups, are pretty much aligned with the local church. There needs to be far more experimentation, perhaps involving several churches, with other ways by which this teaching ministry can be undertaken. The example of the Kirchentag movement in Germany shows that the laity, properly motivated, can be caught up in an enthusiastic encounter with the questions of faith in the modern world. Various lay academies are now functioning and making plain once again that Christian doctrine does not have to be a dry-as-dust affair. Doctrinal study can be an exciting pilgrimage of understanding.

In this connection, the theological seminaries could do far more than they are now doing if they would begin, as some of them have done, to take seriously their task as teaching arms of the church. Faculties could be utilized for the presentation of the best insights of theology to the people of the churches.

No matter how many creative experiments are undertaken, however, the heart of the educational task will remain in the local church. Like so much in the contemporary Christian enterprise, the educational training of the laity is either going to be done in the local church or it probably is not going to be done at all.

Thus, the challenge comes right down to the man in the pastoral ministry, where, we must acknowledge, much of the current trouble is to be found. Amid the welter of responsibilities he faces, the average minister does not take seriously his task as a theologian. Not only does the minister himself shy away from any suggestion that he must be a theologian, but the people of the church would undoubtedly put real theological competence far down the list in any summary of qualities desired in a minister. He is called to be a preacher, but never too heavily theological; he is to be a teacher, but never dryly doctrinal; he is to be a counselor, but never one who lets his theological understanding influence his approach to human beings; he is to be an administrator but never one who tests the program he administers by any kind of theological understanding. What an amazing situation this is — a man whose entire being should be illumined by his theological understanding of God and man but rendered hesitant and apologetic whenever he speaks theologically! It is no wonder, given this sort of a situation, that the modern churches are so often filled with a laity that certainly does not know what it believes, and as a result of this sort of pastoral leadership does not really care very much.

Peter Berger is, I believe, quite right in his assessment of the expectation of the typical congregation. He says:

> The services which this consumers' cooperative in the realm of the spirit [the local congregation] demands of its full-time employee entail, at best, a theological background (in the literal sense of the word) that gives ideological respectability to activities typically unrelated to any theological considerations.[5]

The renewal so urgently sought, then, must first of all come to the men in the pastoral ministry. The minister must be ready to undertake the hard discipline involved in being a theologian. A first step in this direction could well be the recognition that he is going to be a theologian in any case, good or bad, deep or superficial. The suggestion of Martin Marty is in the right direction:

[5] Peter L. Berger, "Religious Establishment and Theological Education," *Theology Today*, Vol. XIX, No. 2, p. 180.

What should a minister *be* in order to change the cultural expectation, reveal his true interest, and be free to serve?

He must be the theologian. Theologian: the worker with the strange task of relating the Word of God to the world of man. He is the scandalous occupant of an offensive vocation: to speak of the unspeakable and to relate himself to the world as one most at home with the finite. "I am no theologian!" many a parson will protest. If he knows what he is saying, he is to be pitied. He is like a white-suited scalpel-wielder who, just before the ether is administered, bends over the patient and says, "Now, I am no surgeon, but. . . ." [6]

Only when he recovers his role as a theologian can the minister restore validity to his vocation or lead the gathered church to a responsible preparation for its witness. Plainly, we are a long way from this as yet. However, there are indications that this type of approach is beginning to be accepted as a valid form of ministry on a wider scale. One result may be the healing of the vocational sickness of the contemporary clergy. Part of this vocational crisis has come about because the clergy have tried to find a reason for being in activities peripheral to their proper concern and, in many instances at least, in doing things which are done much better by others. The suggestion can at least be entertained that ministers will find renewal when they turn back to the proper concerns of the ministry: the conduct of common worship and the education and training of the laity for witness as Christians in the world.

In the light of the concern which is behind these pages, namely, that the church be brought to a recovery of vital ministry in the world, it is important to stress the type of training which I have in mind. The key word here is suggested in a little book by David R. Hunter entitled *Christian Education as Engagement*. He deals in this book with exactly our concern in these reflections, and suggests that

[6] Martin E. Marty, *Second Chance for American Protestants* (New York: Harper & Row, Publishers, Inc., 1963), p. 149.

it is in the concept of engagement that we have a clue to a form of Christian education appropriate for and relevant to today's witness.

Dr. Hunter defines the term engagement as

> the moment when God acts in or upon the life of an individual and the individual faces the obligation to respond. In as much as God is always acting in all life and upon His entire creation, the whole range of one's experience has this theological dimension of engagement. Moreover, since we know from Christian revelation that all experience of this dimension is made possible by God's grace, then the term, in its Christian context, includes the prior action of being met by, being known, being loved by God.[7]

If this concept is taken seriously by the church, certain consequences logically follow. The nurture given its members by the church will have a relevance to the present involvements of the people, and not merely be a preparation for future responsibilities. It will also mean that the task of the church, in its whole witness to the world, will be not merely the transmission of culture but the transformation of culture and hence the training of those who will be the agents of such change. A third implication of this concept is that it makes clear that we are dependent upon grace and thereby are delivered from a Pelagian dependence upon man.

When the church gathers for training, then, it embodies a two-fold purpose:

> 1. It enables us to find our place, provided by God Himself, within that community in which the Holy Spirit lives.
> 2. It is also the first step in training us for carrying out the ministry of reconciliation in the world.[8]

In summary the church must be set free from its inward-looking tendency and begin to look outward toward the world which is the arena of its witness. The task of pre-

[7] David R. Hunter, *Christian Education as Engagement* from Lester Bradner Lectures (New York: The Seabury Press, Inc., 1963), p. 7. Used by permission of Trustees of the Lester Bradner Fund.

[8] *Ibid.*, p. 73.

paring the laity to live as Christians in such a world is the primary responsibility.

III

Basic to any sort of effective witness on the part of the laity is a renewed willingness of the churches to act corporately upon the really pressing matters of our daily existence. If the local church as a whole were to be involved in discussion of current issues, perhaps the problem of the often wide gap between the leadership and members of the church would be alleviated. Too often, the leadership of the church has taken a position on an issue without seriously trying to involve the membership of the congregation in an attempt to understand the situation from a Christian perspective. Such an emphasis upon public affairs would almost dictate that congregations spend less time and effort upon churchly housekeeping so that they may be able to give more of such time and effort to the really important issues of our Christian witness.

In a perceptive article dealing with the life of the so-called "peace churches," J. Lawrence Burkholder makes a strong case for the churches to become discerning communities. He urges that congregations be structured so they may make ethical decisions.

The practical failure of typical congregations in America — including those of the peace churches — to decide and to act corporately is one of the clues to the ethical blandness of Protestantism. Most churches simply do not know how to come to conclusions about things that matter. Nor do they see decision-making as one of the marks of the church. . . . Consensus is seldom sought; discussions are mere forums, and in most cases are not intended to lead to binding commitments; controversial issues are avoided. Dialogical give-and-take, as an instrument of the Holy Spirit, is discouraged by those who prefer "peace" and by those who operate under the illusion that clerical pronouncements are a sufficient substitute for consensus. Is it too harsh to say that most Protestant congregations decide in the course of a year almost nothing of real spiritual importance? . . . Great issues such as war, race, housing, capital punishment, unemployment and the needs of the under-developed countries may be the subjects of sermons, but they do not become existential realities for most churchmen until they are presented as issues concerning which the church must make decisions.[9]

These comments are certainly not too strong an indictment of our existing practice. We have avoided this area of our Christian witness, because we have recognized that debate on such issues would probably do our institutional health no good. So we have skipped these issues, finding a specious security in the consideration of matters of ecclesiastical housekeeping, vaguely troubled because the Christian venture seems drab and unexciting.

The way out of this drabness will exact a cost. However, to become involved in serious discussion of current public issues is a part of our response to the call to go out of the church and into the world with the anguish of our concern. To quote Dr. Burkholder again:

Congregations restructured as discerning communities would concertedly seek to meet specific needs in the world. Ethical involvement would be one of the most important ways in which people of faith answer the call to discipleship. Their particular orientation in the area of ethics would not dispose them to sponsor internal exercises in perfection; rather, the congregation would be ordered around works of love in lowly places. Its eyes would be turned outward.[10]

If this involvement is to take place, it calls for the renewal of the church meeting as the spot at which the gathered community seeks to make its impact felt concerning the vital issues of the day in community, nation, and world, and where the gathered fellowship, under the guidance

[9] J. Lawrence Burkholder, "The Peace Churches as Communities of Discernment," *The Christian Century,* September 4, 1963, p. 1073. Copyright 1963 Christian Century Foundation. Reprinted by permission.
[10] *Ibid.*

of the Holy Spirit, seeks to share its corporate insight into God's will with the members of the congregation. These members bring their perplexities and their dilemmas to the church meeting, share them with their fellow-members, and then together seek to discover the will of God. Then the church meeting will become once again a place of venture where more important matters are faced than the color of paint to be applied to the wall in the nursery.

All of this training and witness would not make the life of the church easy. It would make it significant — and even very exciting.

IV

There is, however, one other aspect of the gathered life of the church which should not be overlooked. In its life together, the church should manifest a deep concern to be the people of God who know one another through meaningful fellowship. We need not be afraid of the word "fellowship," provided that what we have in mind is not a back-slapping joviality but a sense of a people bound to one another by the love of Christ. Then our love and concern for each other in the church becomes the perfectly proper expression of our gratitude to Christ for his action in calling us together in the church.

The sort of Christian witness for which these pages have been pleading is not easy. Bearing such a witness will take a heavy toll upon people who are in a world which is often tough and hard. Backs can grow weary in the bearing of burdens and hearts can be broken in the face of the world's callousness. The church fellowship must be a place of refreshment and renewal where those who bear the heat and burden of witness in the world can come and find others who are ready to share the experience, by offering the friendship which helps to heal the hurts, perhaps by only standing by in Christian love, saying nothing, simply being there and letting one's very presence speak of understanding what the other has been through and of a willingness as far as possible to share in the hurt. This sense of mutual support is what the fellowship of the church can mean.

Let us also remember that life in the church is, in Lionel Thornton's phrase, "the common life in the Body of Christ." Accordingly, we need not fear the more mundane ways by which the Holy Spirit may minister to us in the church. The much-maligned pot-luck supper can on occasion be a sacrament, and the various fellowship groups of the church, even when gathered for play, can fill a vitally important role in our lives. Laughter and gaiety should not, I believe, be strangers in the courts of the Lord's house; they are often ministers of God's grace to heavy human hearts.

Another aspect of the church's life is that the church is called not only to do something but to be something. If its own inner life denies what it outwardly professes, it is a fraud — and the world will recognize it as such. The task of the church in its local reality is to be a judgment upon, not a reflection of, the surrounding culture. The fellowship of the church must be inclusive; it must be the community of acceptance, welcoming in the name of Christ all who seek him, those of one's own race and those of other races, those of one's own class and those of other classes, those who are quite respectable and those whom the rest of society casts out as "unacceptable." Only such a church can be in any real and vital sense the Body of Christ. Only such a church, deep in its commitment to the world, wide in its outreach to people, can be the church in which the Holy Spirit dwells.

Thus, we have the case for the church: the church scattered, the church gathered. It does not bother me at all if you say that you have never seen such a church. Nor have I ever seen such a church in its fullness. But I have seen a vision of what the church can be, and I find it immensely satisfying and thrilling to work, from within the church that now is, to fashion a church which God can use for his mission in the world.

Every person, I believe, confronts a choice at this point. If we want the church renewed, we may work toward this goal either from outside or from within the church. My choice is clear: I believe that the renewal of the church will come, not from those outside venting their indignant judgments upon the church, but from those within who give heart and mind to the task of listening to God's Word for the church, speaking that Word, and endeavoring to shape the life of the church in conformity to that Word. So I believe that renewal will come — in God's time and according to his will.

5

A THEOLOGICAL APPROACH
TO THE MIMEOGRAPH MACHINE

The establishment of the case for the local church is essential, but it is not sufficient. One may be theoretically convinced that the local congregation is indispensable and at the same time feel the terrible futility of much of the pastor's task. The faded luster of the pastoral ministry will not be overcome without a candid look at some of the aspects of the pastoral vocation which at present disturb many and disillusion some.

There are, of course, many such aspects. It is not possible to look at all of them; therefore, in this and the two following chapters I want to consider three which seem to me of particular importance. The first is the whole area of administration; the second is the increasingly tense situation experienced when the ministry seems to be leading the church into an ever-deeper involvement in social issues; and the third is the difficulty experienced in exercising ministry in an interim period when old landmarks have vanished and new guidelines are very slow in emerging. It is highly unlikely that the sense of "privilege" can be restored unless some way is found of living creatively with these "burdens."

I

There is little doubt that many men in the pastoral ministry find administration a burden which all but obliterates the privilege. Hosts of ministers find themselves forced by the structure of the church into the assumption of administrative duties which keep them from doing the things they really feel to be important.

A clear indication of this burden is in the action of Dr. Lowell Russell Ditzen in resigning his position as senior minister of the Reformed Church of Bronxville, New York, one of the great parishes of America. No matter what criteria are used to judge it, this church is an imposing phenomenon. Located in prosperous Westchester County, the church has over 3,400 members. On its staff at the time of Dr. Ditzen's resignation were five ministers, all of them capable and well-trained; each man specialized in a certain area of the parish work. Despite its size and complexity, the church is well organized and more than adequately supported by a host of loyal laymen. Viewed in terms of our usual American "success" mentality, it would seem that to be minister of such a church would be the peak of one's career.

For twelve years Dr. Ditzen was the minister of this church. He was successful in his work and greatly loved by the people of the church. On August 31, 1962, he resigned his position.

The natural question is, why? We obviously cannot look into the mind of Dr. Ditzen nor search his heart. But we can find at least part of the reason for the resignation in the words he used in his farewell correspondence to his congregation. Here, in part, is what he said in explanation:

> It can be put in one sentence: I am convinced it is God's will. First, as a minister I am committed to the way of spiritual and intellectual growth. Only so can I, or any clergyman, adequately fulfill his role of spiritual guide. Now in the church that has grown

about us, numbering some 3,400 souls, with the ever-increasing administrative demands and calls for a personal ministry to people with wide-varied problems, the first matter is increasingly pushed in the background. I would not be fair to my calling or to you to continue a program that progressively prohibits my doing "first things."

Secondly, I am aware that our generation is facing more ominous days than when I completed my graduate studies twenty-five years ago. Our great Protestant churches are not fulfilling, with power and light, their roles. Why? One reason is that clergymen, like myself, have become bound by the web of "programs and mechanics," till they have no time to be quiet and hear "the still small voice.". . .

Thirdly, I am deeply concerned about our nation. America has a destiny in history. Yet our religious trumpets are giving an uncertain sound. America and Americans are not being called to the high road of personal responsibility, integrity and vision on which we should be walking. Again, why? Because religious leaders, like myself, do not have the time to drink from the fountains of our origin, to study the real issues of the present and so to inspire us to greatness by prophetic utterance. I do not say I will find the answers. I only know I must try.[1]

Let the minister who has never known the same impulse cast the first innuendo! My purpose in drawing attention to Dr. Ditzen's resignation, however, is neither to praise him nor to blame him. Rather, I cite this as one more bit of evidence that there is something seriously wrong in the approach to his work taken by the average contemporary parish minister.

We have already looked in some detail at the crisis in pastoral morale. Books and articles dealing with it continue to be written and published. No one who is at all close to the current group of pastors can be unaware of the reality of this crisis.

Occasionally, of course, one may be tempted to point out

[1] Quoted by Kyle Haselden, "In Search of Arabia," *The Pulpit,* Vol. XXXIII, No. 10 (October, 1962), p. 3. Copyright 1962 Christian Century Foundation. Reprinted by permission.

that the ministry is not the only profession undergoing this sort of critical self-examination. The medical and legal professions are very much involved in the same type of anxious examination of themselves, and other professions face the problem only in a slightly less serious form. So those in the pastoral ministry need to be on guard lest they assume that only *their* vocational role is filled with perplexity. There is a real temptation for the parish clergy to join in a kind of professional lament, exceeding every other professional group in their capacity for feeling sorry for themselves. To listen to some of the current conversation among pastors — a dismaying discipline at times — is to have the eerie feeling that everybody else has a nice, safe, easy, comfortable job. Pastors are the most overworked and underpaid group in the nation. Their job, they insist, is an utterly impossible one. Churches want as pastors men who combine intellectual penetration with a folksy manner, spiritual depth with man-of-the-world sophistication, administrative know-how with other-worldly piety. They want, in short, a kind of man who never existed. In the South, as someone has said, every pulpit committee looks for a Confederate veteran under thirty-five years of age! So the complaints run on and on, and there is danger in adding to them. A balance somehow has to be achieved between self-pity and a clear-eyed recognition that there are, after all, some real problems and difficulties involved in trying to be a faithful parish minister today. What is sought is not some magical way by which to make the vocation easy; this is both impossible and unworthy. On the contrary, what is urgently needed is some understanding of the ministry which will include the hardships as part of the total vocation and be so recognized within a minister's commitment to his calling.

One refrain runs through all current discussions about the ministry. This refrain stresses the contention that the role of the minister has undergone a tremendous change in the past few decades. There was a time when the minister could encompass his task in two words: preacher and pastor. To be sure, there may have been other tasks as well which he was expected to carry out, but those tasks were minor in their demands on his time and energy. It is always dangerous, of course, to idolize the past; there was probably a problem of the ministry then as well as now. Even realizing this danger, it must be granted, I believe, that the ministry today is a far different calling and in some ways a far more demanding calling than in days gone by.

The chief reason for this increase in difficulty is that the role of the parish minister has expanded. The old twofold division of labor just doesn't fit today. The pastor today confronts at least a sixfold division of his task. He is, as Samuel Blizzard's study makes plain, administrator, organizer, pastor, preacher, priest, and teacher. The source of conflict in the pastoral calling is found in the clash which is claimed to exist between the minister's own image of his role and that of the laymen in the church. The duties considered most important by the minister are considered least important by the laymen and vice versa. Such a situation obviously has all the makings of a tension-filled vocational experience.

The conflict comes into clearest focus at the point of administration and organization. Every minister is aware that the demands in these two areas have vastly increased. A large portion of the time of ministers must be spent today in tasks having to do with either administration or organization. The average church is a veritable beehive of activity, and the competition among denominations means that each church feels a compulsion to offer a program which can compete with that of other churches, although we usually prefer to put the matter in a more polite manner. This situation means that the parish minister must keep the wheels humming and the groups moving — the direction of less importance than the fact of movement.

When the minister must thus give time to what he secretly believes to be activities of dubious worth, he feels a real conflict within himself. The source of tension arises from the fact that the minister has no coherent theory or theology which relates his different tasks to one another and to his total vocation in a meaningful way. His theology may be sound enough in its doctrinal emphases, but it does not provide an adequate perspective by which he can gain guidance in the perplexing welter of duties he confronts. James Gustafson, who worked with H. Richard Niebuhr in the study of the ministry, defines the problem of the minister as:

> that of determining *who he is* and *what he is doing* within the complexity of his functions. He frequently lacks, more than anything else, an awareness of what he is about, and therefore he has no central focus for the integration of his various activities.[2]

Since this integrating viewpoint is precisely what is missing today, the minister finds himself inwardly rebelling at his administrative burden. This rebellion has, I believe, many causes, some of them more legitimate than others. Let's look first at some of the less admirable reasons for the ministerial rebellion against administrative tasks.

II

First of all, many persons have trouble with administration simply because they do not seem to be gifted with administrative ability. They would find it difficult to carry through tasks whether they were ministers in the church or employees in a business. The basic principles of sound administration, many of which are simply commonsense rules of procedure, are mysteries to them. Consequently, they feel lost and adrift in the administrative wilderness piled upon their desks.

[2] James Gustafson, "An Analysis of the Problem of the Role of the Minister," *The Journal of Religion,* Vol. XXXIV, No. 3, p. 187.

In defense of pastors like these we might point out that they never started out in the ministry with any idea that they were administrative dynamos; few ever reckoned seriously with the possibility that they would have much to do in the way of administration. As a result, they developed an image of themselves as prophets, standing in the prophetic succession of the Old Testament, ardently championing the downtrodden and the oppressed; as preachers of the gospel, setting forth in clear language the claims of Christ upon men today; as priests, leading people in the venture of common worship; and as pastors, sharing with people their joys and sorrows, victories and defeats. There was little room indeed in such an image of the ministry for the harried man who sits almost hidden behind a desk piled high with papers, immersed in matters of budgets and leaky roofs, trying to get down on paper an organizational chart of his church which will help him to make sense of an organization which has, like Topsy, just grown up around him. In the days when he was getting ready to venture out in the parish ministry, his mind was filled with great issues of theology, and administration was something he was content to leave to bishops and executive secretaries, many of whom he felt, richly deserved such a fate.

If a minister could live over those days of preparation with the wisdom gained by hindsight, he might be interested somewhere along the line in some study of good administrative procedure. This would not, of course, have solved all his problems, but it might have lessened the intolerable frustration which his ineptness as an administrator creates. There is more than a modicum of truth in William H. Hudnut's contention in his *Christian Century* article entitled "Are Ministers Cracking Up?" in which he writes:

> Sometimes he is a poor organizer, and has to pay the same penalties as any other poor organizer. . . . Sometimes, courting the limelight, he overloads his schedule, puts second or third things

first and finds himself far behind in the necessary matters. Sometimes, in short, he cracks up because he has not had the discipline to crack down on himself.[3]

Part of what is involved in this cracking down would be the mastering of the rudiments of good administrative procedures, thereby freeing the minister from the frustrations produced by ineptitude.

There is a second reason for the administrative burden the modern minister faces. Here, too, the fault lies at least in part with the minister, because it is found in the theory under which many ministers seem to operate. The theory might be called the myth of indispensability. Part of the reason for the growth of administrative pressure is found in the determination on the part of the minister to retain the operation of the church in his own hands. For reasons we shall look at in a moment, the minister refuses to delegate responsibility for phases of the church's program or operation to the laity. This is a problem which has, as far as I can discover, little to do with varieties of church polity. Even in churches of the congregational order, which are theoretically most open to lay leadership, the problem is present. Instead of seeking to involve laymen in the affairs of the church, thereby strengthening the church, ministers tend to keep the reins firmly in their own hands; and then wonder why the church resembles a runaway wagon, careening along with the clergyman bounced this way and that as he tries to retain his precarious position.

Very definitely, the reason for the delegation of tasks in the church is not primarily to lessen the burden on the minister; such an aim would be unwise and unworthy. The reason is twofold: for the sake of the church itself and for the sake of the laymen. The task of the church is to be the

[3] William H. Hudnut, Jr., "Are Ministers Cracking Up?" *The Christian Century*, Vol. 73 (November 7, 1956), p. 1288. Copyright 1956 Christian Century Foundation. Reprinted by permission.

ministering community. In the name of our Lord the church seeks to live its life in the posture of a servant. In carrying out this commission, the church has need of Christians with differing gifts. These gifts, whatever they may be, are then brought to the church to be exercised in the life of the church in such a manner as to help the church fulfill its ministering role. The layman does have gifts which the church needs, many gifts of many different sorts. He can make his contribution toward the ministering nature of the church by the employment of his gifts in such fashion as to free others for their particular type of ministry. Let it be emphasized, however, that this is not the whole extent of the layman's witness; it is only to say that he can give valuable and often expert help in the administrative operation of the church. The "diversities of gifts" of which Paul speaks apply at this point, and the minister is foolish and inefficient who does not seek to utilize these diverse gifts. More than this is involved. It was Paul who also pointed out that "these were his gifts: some to be apostles, some prophets, some evangelists, some pastors and teachers, to equip God's people for work in his service, to the building up of the body of Christ" (Ephesians 4:11, 12, NEB). A primary task in the church is thus to "equip God's people for work in his service," and in that job the laymen can make a tremendously important contribution, provided that they are utilized by the minister.

Actually, of course, behind the failure to delegate responsibility lurks a fear, not often expressed but nevertheless present. If ministers put aside as quite unworthy the desire for power itself — a sin to which ministers, being human, are just as prone as other men — they must admit that too often they are not sufficiently confident of their own ability to risk working closely with laymen. They seem to suspect that the laymen, if permitted access to the detailed workings of the church, may emerge less than enthusiastic about the minister's abilities in various realms. Ignorance on the part of the laymen may not be bliss, but it is security for the minister. Hence the minister, not quite sure of himself in relation to his laymen, seeks safety and security in the myth of indispensability, giving the impression that nothing in the church can get done well unless he personally takes care of it. Surely, however, such an attitude is a devastating commentary upon the ties that are supposed to bind minister and laymen in the life of the church and an equally tragic failure of the minister to use every person and every technique which will "equip God's people for work in his service."

Not all the reasons for the tension concerning administration are as bad as the two thus far advanced. There are some good reasons for our concern with the problem.

The resignation of Dr. Ditzen was motivated at least in part by a conviction that his administrative burden progressively prohibited him from doing some "first things." There is no mystery among ministers as to what this means. The first things concern the deeper dimensions of their task. It is a matter of genuine concern when the organization and administration of the church get in the way of careful attention to more important things.

To be specific, all of those in the parish ministry recognize that their habits of study can easily degenerate, until their reading is done in odd moments and consists largely of the sermonic efforts of their colleagues. Real study is left behind, a memory of days in seminary. Meanwhile, as the days fly past, they promise themselves that they are going to make time for some serious studying. But then this matter arises and that committee meets and the other board gets into a snarl, and they bid a reluctant farewell to the promised wrestling with Barth and Tillich, Niebuhr and Bultmann. The books on their shelves are mute and inarticulate; the people on the committees are vociferous and demanding. Pastors therefore give their attention to the loud voices and an embarrassed apology to their books.

The resulting impoverishment of the pastoral ministry is familiar enough. Dimly we perceive that without earnest study, without anguished wrestling with the deeper issues of Christian thought and life, ministers can have no kindling word to speak and no relevant guidance to give. But they are caught, seemingly the helpless prisoners of "the system."

Not only does their study suffer, but their work with persons also suffers. One of the marks of the effective parish minister is the sense he gives people of available time. He should be unhurried in his approach to his people, resolved to give them the impression that nothing in the world is more important to him than the problem or perplexity they bring him. Despite the honest desire of the parish minister to be able to give this sort of undistracted attention to his people, he is often under such pressure that he gives his people the unconscious impression that they are intruding upon his precious time. I repeat that this is not the minister's intention; it is far from his desire; most of the parish ministers I know are men with a genuine desire to be of help to people. But no matter what the intention or desire, he often finds that the administrative burden forces him to be on the move all the time, and such pressure prohibits effective ministry to persons.

Basic to this concern is the tension felt by many parish ministers between the calling of the church to mission and the demands of the church as institution. When so much of a man's time is consumed by housekeeping activities, he feels the terrible thrust of the irrelevance of his work to the vast issues of man's life today. If this concern is felt by parish ministers, it is the subject of vehement protest by many Christian young people. The pathetic irrelevance of the church to the deeper issues of human life and destiny, the failure of the church to be in any real sense the pilgrim people of God, the timidity of the church before crucial issues, the introverted self-love of the church instead of outgoing love of man — these features of the modern church have created in the minds of many sincere Christian young people a questioning about the church's place in the purpose of God.

This concern was given strong expression at the World Teaching Conference of the World Student Christian Federation held in Strasbourg, France, in the summer of 1960. The theme was "The Life and Mission of the Church," and one student delegate, reporting on the conference, wrote:

> Rejection of the institutional Church came through strongly at Strasbourg. In the opening address, Richard Shaull described the structures of the church as obsolete. Parish life operates on the periphery of human life rather than at its center. Mission boards pre-suppose a concept of missions that is no longer valid. . . . The language that the Church uses, often unrelated to the life situation of the common man, was found out of date and wanting. The self-love of the Church institutional, its concern about its own life and constant pointing to itself rather than to Christ when indicating where there is life and hope, seemed a direct contradiction of the Church as the Body of Christ.[4]

This indictment may, of course, be put down as the typical impatience of young people and so dismissed. Yet many parish ministers feel very much the same. They may not be so vehement, but they are fully as disturbed.

Some 51 percent of the time of the parish minister, according to Samuel Blizzard's study, is spent in administrative or organizational work. This time cannot then be given to other tasks. The church as institution thus gets in the way of the church as mission, and the parish minister, deeply concerned about the mission of the church, finds himself caught in an intolerable situation. The result is inward chafing and restlessness.

Most of us, whatever our own approach to this matter, can feel a degree of sympathy for the young minister in

[4] *The Student World*, Quarterly Magazine of the World Student Christian Foundation, No. 1-2 (1961), p. 206.

his hot impatience with the institutional church. Walter Wagoner, who as director of the Rockefeller Theological Fellowship Programs was in close contact with many young ministers, quotes a letter from one of them. The young minister wrote:

> I intend to spend my ministry disorganizing churches, by which I mean eliminating all committees and meetings I can that are not absolutely necessary to run the church. I'm pretty sure most churches could get along fine on about half of the organization they now have. . . . With this extra free time I would then concentrate on small-group discussion and prayer and Bible work.[5]

These, then, are some of the reasons, as I see it, for the emerging concern about administration in the life of the parish minister — the lack of administrative skill, the myth of indispensability, the frustration produced by diversion from what are believed to be basic matters to what are considered peripheral concerns, and the conflict between the church as mission and the church as institution. Other reasons could doubtless be added, but let these suffice to outline the problem before us in some of its sharp dimensions.

III

What, then, can be done about the dilemma of administration? One thing seems perfectly clear: no matter what changes may be effected in the church's life, there will be no magical way by which the administrative task can suddenly be waved away. It will continue to demand a large portion of the time and energy of the parish minister.

This being the case, ministers have only two choices before them. One is to continue as at present, doing the administrative work but inwardly rebelling against it; the

[5] Quoted in Walter D. Wagoner, "One for the Ministry, Two to Go," *Religion in Life,* Vol. 31 (Autumn, 1962), p. 514.

other is to seek a total understanding of the parish ministry which will include within its scope the task of administration. If they can achieve this kind of outlook — what I have called a theological approach to the mimeograph machine — they may be delivered from some of their frustration and perhaps also see the total life of the church in a more wholesome manner.

When we try to come to grips with the larger problem of the ministry, there are really two contradictory urges at war within us. One is the urge to flight, the other the urge to involvement. One way seeks redemption apart from the world, the other redemption in the world. One seeks the blessed vision of God in private ecstacy, the other seeks the vision of God in the pulsating, throbbing realities of daily existence. One way leads ultimately to the monastery, the other ever deeper into the tangled life of the workaday world. These contrasting urges are sometimes referred to as the Catholic and Protestant urges respectively, but I think they are more truly understood as urges within each believing Christian. With part of himself the Christian is tempted to flee from the complexities and perplexities of the world to a quiet haven, where he can center his attention upon the reality of God; with another part of himself he feels drawn toward the aching need of the world and feels the call of God to serve precisely in the tangled realities of man's ordinary existence.

This tension between engagement and withdrawal has been used by Gabriel Fackre as a way to come to an understanding of the work of ministry in our day. After serving a church in the stockyards area of Chicago, he became pastor of Grace Evangelical and Reformed Church in Duquesne, Pennsylvania, and Mount Zion Community Church in West Mifflin, also in Pennsylvania. Out of his experience he wrote a little book entitled *The Purpose and Work of the Ministry*. Slight in size and modest in scope, the book is full of insight into the meaning of ministry.

Mr. Fackre draws a contrast between his orientation as a Protestant mission pastor and the monastic vocation of Thomas Merton. He dramatizes this contrast in terms of the image of the "Waters of Siloe," symbolizing the quiet, cloistered Christian obedience of Thomas Merton in the Trappist Monastery in Gethsemani, Kentucky, and the "River of God," symbolizing the immersion of the mission pastor in the moving, often turbulent, currents of our common humanity. It is an illuminating contrast.[6]

There is little mystery about the monastic ideal of a way of life based upon a conviction that the love of God is most perfectly expressed in a life radically separated from the throes of ordinary daily existence. The main thrust of the contemplative ideal is expressed in Merton's own words:

> There were still men on this miserable, noisy, cruel earth, who tasted the marvelous joy of silence and solitude, who dwelt in forgotten mountain cells, in secluded monasteries, where the news and desires and appetites and conflicts of the world no longer reached them.
>
> They were free from the burden of flesh's tyranny, and their clear vision, clean of the world's smoke and its bitter sting, were raised to heaven and penetrated into the deeps of heaven's infinite and healing light.[7]

Even if one must continue to live in the world, the ideal is to keep as clear as possible from newspapers, radio, and other distractions of this mortal life. The very contradiction that a person feels between the noise of the world and his desire to be alone can be accepted "as a seed of solitude" [8] which will keep him alert to opportunities to be alone in silence in the presence of God. In short, then, the monastic

[6] Gabriel Fackre, *The Purpose and Work of the Ministry* (Philadelphia: United Church Press, 1959), pp. 9-10. Used by permission of the United Church Press.

[7] Thomas Merton, *The Seven Storey Mountain,* (New York: Harcourt, Brace & World, Inc., 1948), p. 316.

[8] Thomas Merton, *Seeds of Contemplation,* (New York: Dell Publishing Co., Inc., 1949), p. 54.

ideal, undistracted contemplation by the "Waters of Siloe," calls for the breaking of all ties to earth. It is necessary to get far from "the world's smoke and its bitter sting."

On the other hand, the task of the minister, summoned by God to journey on the river of time, called to involvement in the world for the sake of the gospel, is radically different. This vocation takes with the utmost seriousness the biblical conviction that God is Lord of history and that he is therefore encountered, not alone in quiet and secluded mountain cells, but *especially* in the frantic, rushing world of common life. The consistent witness of the Scriptures is to a God who meets man in the elemental experiences of daily life — in his work and his worship, in his play and his prayer, in his politics and his piety. This means that the minister is one who is called, in the words of Mr. Fackre:

> to feel in one's own being the bruises and cuts of the workaday world, and to strive to serve as an instrument of their healing. It is to take up one's life stance . . . in the place where men live out their lives, and not to flee into some protected cove, insulated from the tensions and perplexities of modern society. It is to company with people in the "really real" experiences of birth and death, joy and anxiety, to face and to share elemental concerns of human life like going to the hospital, like the fears of a mother, like the good intentions of a convert, like the ways and means of earning one's bread, and to believe that these concerns are not beneath the dignity of God, and therefore, certainly not of his undershepherds. It is to accept as a rightful part of shepherding common work with hands and back, like painting basement walls with the men of the church, or planting trees at a campsite with the youth, or setting up tables with the women for a church supper. It is to find such devices of temporality as a telephone or slide projector, or a mimeograph to be legitimate and worthwhile tools for holy work.[9]

Such an approach as this sketched out of the experience of a mission pastor indicates that we must be careful lest we become overly "spiritual" in our assessment of the means God uses for the accomplishment of his purpose.

[9] Gabriel Fackre, *op. cit.*, pp. 10-11.

There are clear implications in this understanding of the ministry for administration. The work of the parish minister is bound up with the people of the parish. Together in a host of ways minister and people seek to live and work in such fashion that the church is enabled to be a ministering community. If this task is to be effectively carried out, it means that parish ministers dare not seek a cloistered piety. It means that in the seemingly mundane tasks of administration they have an opportunity to show how the gospel meets the needs of modern man. By taking administration in this fashion and making it part of their total ministry, pastors may see where this onerous task can take on new, deeper, and more creative meaning.

Consider briefly just a couple of positive possibilities for administration, from the point of view of the parish minister interested in the Christian growth and witness of the people of the church. Administration provides an opportunity and a setting for the minister and people to express their faith in personal relationships. The raising of the church budget, an exceedingly dreary chore in many ways, provides a wonderfully effective way by which to lead people to a new sense of values. What is the church on earth to do and to be? Where can such a question be more directly faced than in terms of the allocation of the church's money? Precisely at this point the parish really indicates what it considers its mission to be. Sermons and study groups dealing with mission in somewhat abstract terms are valuable adjuncts, but some of the most creative implementation of mission can be achieved through the help of a pastor who is aware that the church determines mission, not by votes or resolutions or idealistic pronouncements, but by the way it spends its money. If most of the congregation's concern is introverted, the question of mission is, for all practical purposes, stifled. If more of the resources of the church are allocated in outward service to the community and the world, something very different is said about mission. The pastor who looks upon the church budget as a "materialistic" matter and therefore beneath his lofty notice has overlooked an exceedingly important strategic possibility.

Or, when a church is considering its activities for the coming year, what should be emphasized? What does the church want to see accomplished in its community and in the world? How can the parish minister face these questions better than in the committees wrestling with the programs of the women's group, the men's council, the youth fellowship? If the women's group would give consideration to such matters as the community responsibility of the congregation, to the church's concern for the racial revolution, or to what women can actually do about the youth of the area, their activities would be rescued from futility. In such meetings, too often seen as a burden, the pastor has the privilege of sharing in real personal relationships with people who are trying, as the minister himself is also trying, to see what Christian living means for the church and for Christians. These administrative areas are rich indeed in teaching opportunities.

Notice, furthermore, that this burden of administration provides the parish minister with a real opportunity to come to grips with the kind of experience many laymen face all the time. Dreary monotony is a real part of much modern work. Hosts of laymen chafe at this and wonder what faith has to do with daily work. The parish minister who cannot relate his own faith creatively to the problems of drudgery and monotony has little right to preach an eloquent sermon calling laymen to serve God in their daily work. Here, at least, the minister is on common footing with his laymen, and the burden of administration is an opportunity to share in the layman's dilemma and to indicate, in a conviction born out of experience, that faith does have something of indispensable value to contribute to daily work.

Such an approach as that sketchily outlined here will not

make the parish ministry an easy calling. It has never been that; it never, please God, will be that. As Paul W. Hoon said:

> No, the problem of the Protestant clergy today is not how to make the ministry more possible. The problem is how to live as redeemed and redeeming men with its impossibility. . . .
>
> The minister proclaims justification. Does he also know God's mercy to his own life, forgiving him in the midst of tasks undone for their "undoneness," accepting him in his unprofitableness, filling up out of the divine fullness his emptiness, completing his brokenness and healing his distraction with peace? [10]

Somewhere in the hidden and mysterious depths of the minister's life in God will be found the grace to accept the burdens with faithfulness and the privileges with joy.

[10] Paul Waitman Hoon, "Building Up Breaking-Down Parsons," *The Christian Century*, Vol. 74 (November 6, 1957), p. 1314. Copyright 1957 Christian Century Foundation. Reprinted by permission.

6

PASTOR AND PEOPLE:
A FEW GROUND RULES

Partly as a result of the wholesome interest of the contemporary ministry for a faith that will be relevant to the vexing issues of the social order, clergymen have moved to the front ranks of those seriously questioning some aspects of the social order and insistently demanding far-reaching and radical changes. Such a ministry has opened a gap between many pastors and people of the congregation. No longer does the church convey the image of a nice, complacent, comfortable institution, happy in having made its peace with society. Not only is it characterized by the sounds of hymns and prayers and sermons, but also by debate and discussion, often rising to acrimonious levels, as the search goes on for faithfulness in mission. In short, the future is going to disclose that the church is both a center of controversy and a scene of conflict when it faces crucial social issues.

Controversy occurs precisely because many ministers and some laymen have taken seriously the challenge embodied in the concept of the scattered church dispersed into society as an agent of social change. This concept, inescapable as I believe it to be, comes with a high price tag attached.

No longer is the church the community of peace and quiet. The church becomes the center of conflict.

The man concerned about the pastoral ministry had better reckon with the reality of the cost of conflict. He may theoretically and enthusiastically adopt the image of the scattered congregation and rejoice in the social activism to which he is convinced Christian faith summons him and the church. He may even make his peace with the administrative demands of the institution. But he is going to be in for real trouble unless he faces up to the fact that the images of both the church and the pastor are going to be seriously changed in the next couple of decades. The change will be in the direction of associating both the institution and the pastor with conflict. The radical nature of this revolutionary change in the concept of the pastor, both as held by the laity and by the pastor himself, can be appreciated only if it is set over against the image almost generally accepted a few years ago. Gone is the beneficent, kindly, inoffensive figure of the pastor. The "New Breed" of pastor has emerged, and whatever else he has brought with him, there has certainly come a recognition that conflict within the church and beyond it is an inescapable part of contemporary ministry.

I

The signs of this new turmoil are visible on every hand. "I expect to be involved in conflict," said a young minister in Rochester, New York, "the rest of my life."[1]

According to Harvey Cox:

The New Breed has brought to the fore a style of theology and a political vision that have lain dormant for some years although they have deep sources in the Christian tradition and in the American religious experience. In Buffalo, Philadelphia, Kansas City,

[1] Quoted in William C. Martin, "Shepherds Vs. Flocks: Ministers and Negro Militancy," *The Atlantic,* December, 1967, p. 59. Copyright 1967, William C. Martin, used by permission.

Chicago, Oakland, and dozens of others cities, the New Breed can be found organizing welfare unions, tenants' councils, rent strikes, and school boycotts. Wherever they are at work, they have evoked opposition, both inside and outside the churches. The resulting tensions have made church politics livelier and more interesting today than they have been for decades.[2]

The New Yorker caught the spirit of the contemporary church in a cartoon. Out of the church, obviously ejected forcibly, went the minister. The cartoon's caption read: "He really must have stepped on some toes today."

Toes have been stepped on all over the American church scene. The yelps of pain have been reflected in the secular press, with many accounts from different localities but all of them telling essentially the same story: "Minister asked to leave his church in controversy over social policy." The headline hides much anguish, glosses over many bitter feelings, and does not really get at the depth of the problem now facing the church's ministry and laity. *Life* magazine described this phenomenon in the blunt title of an article analyzing five cases of pastors in some degree of trouble in their parishes: "Crunch in the Churches." The pastor is the one caught in that "crunch," and the experience can be a harrowing one indeed.

The problem is found in the fact that a myth has been exploded. The myth is that of clergy-laity unanimity. Now, to be sure, this unanimity was never complete, and through the centuries from New Testament times to this era the history of the church has been filled with tensions and conflicts. But there has been a significant change in the nature and context of the conflict in our day. In the past, the conflict often involved a jockeying for positions of power, a desire for domination by laymen of minister or

[2] Harvey G. Cox, "The 'New Breed' in American Churches: Sources of Social Activism in American Religion," *Daedalus*, Vol. 96, No. 1 (Winter, 1967), p. 136. Reprinted by permission from *Daedalus*, Journal of the American Academy of Arts and Sciences, Boston, Massachusetts.

minister of laymen; a disagreement over procedures for the setting of priorities, laymen having one idea and the minister another; or over matters of policy, touching on any one of many aspects of the church's housekeeping operations; and sometimes the conflict centered in worthwhile, if frequently too bitter, conflicts over theological issues. These were often dismaying, frequently disrupting, and, for the minister, emotionally and literally moving experiences. While such church conflicts were always deplorable, they were not quite the same as the conflicts we now confront. For they were held within a context of agreement on the basic purposes of the church itself. The differences were likely to be over means, not ends; and hence the disagreement was not at a fundamental level.

What makes the current situation so serious is that the conflict between pastor and people has moved to a basic level. Not just means are being questioned today; rather, a radically new perspective on the purpose of the church is at issue. Pastor and people, though bound in the fellowship of the church, have come to look at the basic purpose of the church in different ways and to judge the effectiveness of the congregation in the light of very differing standards. The old context of common presuppositions has disappeared in the process, and the result is that the disagreement becomes more threatening than ever.

It is true, of course, that not all pastors share in the outlook of the New Breed. Many of them find such persons to be puzzling and dismaying people. It is also true that there are many laymen who are open to the new currents and impatient to see the church break out of its former ways and to confront in exciting and dangerous fashion the challenges of today. Nevertheless, the reality of a cleavage is too clear to be denied and too potentially disruptive to be politely glossed over.

There is, however, great reluctance to admit the reality of this tension. Partly, this unwillingness may stem from a feeling that tension and conflict are somehow out of place in the church. The church, according to this view, should be characterized by a benign goodwill on the part of all members toward each other. Those who hold this viewpoint believe that a significant part of the pastor's role is to create and to maintain precisely this kind of good feeling. Any departure from the good feeling is, therefore, an indication of failure on the pastor's part. The tendency we confront is one of denying the reality of the conflict in order to preserve the illusion of successful ministry.

If I am right in this belief that there is a conflict between pastor and people, such disagreement must be brought honestly into the open. There are real perils in the perpetuation of the myth of unanimity. The first step, perhaps, in the restoration of healthy congregational life would be an honest facing of the actual situation. Until this is done, we shall go on perpetuating the myth that the successful pastor is one who can forever escape tension with his congregation. Furthermore, we shall continue to sow the seeds of disillusionment in younger ministers, for whom we shall have set forth an ideal of the pastoral role which can never be fulfilled by a man who seeks honestly to be a minister of God's Word. When the ideal we have taught him to cherish turns out to be both impossible and unworthy, the result is bound to be the disillusionment with the pastoral ministry which is now so evident. The exodus from the pastorate is already great and threatens to grow greater; and we do little to avert the exodus by our pretense that the absence of conflict is a sign of spiritual vitality.

II

Once this conflict is openly admitted, it must be dealt with in some fashion. Certain possibilities are open for the pastor.

One is the way of capitulation. Involved in this is the

familiar spectacle of the emergence of the clergyman and the passing of the minister. Out of a recognition of the reality of the conflict and a desire for its resolution, the pastor determines that the focus of his life is to be the welfare of the institution. A careful nurture of this institution is his life, and to build it up is his responsibility and privilege. In this context the clergyman is defined as one who is oriented to the church as institution and does not want anything to disrupt its smooth functioning.

There are real advantages in that such an approach does away with a great part of the tension and conflict. It is, also, a great deal easier to train men for careers as clergymen than for service as ministers. As Keith Bridston and Dwight Culver point out, "it is easier to describe what a clergyman is, what is required of him, what his training should be, than to define a 'minister.'"[3] The way of capitulation will constantly beckon, and many men will choose that way. What seems very clear now is the need for ministers, not clergymen, for those whom John Donne called "sonnes of thunder" instead of tame and decorous oilers of ecclesiastical machinery.

If the pastor's response to this conflict is not capitulation, it is often frustration. Today the pastor is often required to reconsider very seriously his image of himself. The need is reflected in another comment by a Rochester minister, growing out of the turmoil created by the participation of churches and pastors in the racial struggle in that city. This young man said:

> I came out of seminary with the idea of helping people. I had some avant-garde ideas and I realized some people would resist them, but I had no image of people trying to sink both me and the church. It raises hell with a guy's feeling to have his self-image of Friend and Helper swapped for Enemy of the People.[4]

[3] Keith R. Bridston and Dwight W. Culver, *The Making of Ministers* (Minneapolis: Augsburg Publishing House, 1964), p. viii.

[4] Martin, *op. cit.*, p. 57.

This radical change in images is the difficulty today, and it is no surprise, given the turbulent nature of the times, that there is so much frustration.

In some instances, the frustration leads to a rather total disillusionment. Many men go out of the pastoral ministry, and young men look at the vocation with considerable skepticism. When over 70 percent of the students enrolled in AATS seminaries (American Association of Theological Schools) state that they do not expect to be in the pastorate ten years after ordination, some indication of the gravity of the problem is realized. Add to this number the steady stream of men who get so frustrated they become fed up and get out even after many years of pastoral ministry, and the full dimensions of the problem of recruitment and of the maintenance of the morale of men now in the pastoral ministry can be seen.

The men who leave can be counted. How can we even begin to estimate the number who, for whatever reasons, remain in the vocation but lose the zest and joy of the task? Unable to capitulate, still intent on being ministers of the Word, they pay the price in inner tension and outer sadness. Often lonely, estranged from the fellowship which should be supportive, they are the nameless and unsung heroes of the spiritual struggle of this day.

What emerges from this discussion is a clear recognition that the Christian community can afford neither increased capitulation nor continued frustration. The situation demands an examination of the areas of pastor-people tension and the setting of some ground rules. This task will require wrestling with basic issues regarding the purpose of the church and a courageous willingness on the part of pastor and people to run the risks of honestly confronting each other. It will also require the rigorous questioning of many ideas so long established among us that they have become unconscious assumptions. The whole process may prove extremely painful and involve considerable disruption, but

I know of no easier way by which to deal with a critical situation.

III

Although there are many areas of tension between pastor and people in our churches, I want to look at three briefly, endeavoring to describe the source of the tension and to suggest some ground rules for working in these areas.

Common to all these areas of tension is a serious difference between the way pastors, especially the younger men, and lay people think about the basic purpose of the church. A very significant change is under way in this area, and while the new emphasis is not entirely without problems or dangers, it is nevertheless a fact that the new way of thinking has been endorsed by many. This change in the understanding of the basic purpose of the church is all tied up with the new thrust toward a worldly theology. This new theology includes a recognition that the church is not in existence for its own self-aggrandizement. The church cannot live with its eye upon its own welfare exclusively. No longer can the church conceive of its basic task as snatching people from a worldly to a churchly existence. To increase the love of God and neighbor, as H. Richard Niebuhr put it, is the basic purpose of the church.[5]

Perhaps for the sake of convenience the change can be described in terms of three progressions, all of them generally accepted by the new generation of pastors but encountering some degree of opposition from the people of the churches. The church is moving from the inward to the outward as its sphere of mission, from success to service as its criterion of mission, from support to disturbance as its mode of mission. Each of these progressions involves a shift in the traditional interpretation of the church's purpose, and

[5] H. Richard Niebuhr, *The Purpose of the Church and Its Ministry* (New York: Harper & Row, Publishers, Inc., 1956), p. 27.

as a result each progression leads to either a widening of the chasm between pastor and people or a deepened awareness of God's mission for the church now.

Not so long ago it was widely accepted that the church's basic mission was to build up its own life. Most of the energy and time of pastors could be given to the cultivation of the spiritual interests of the church's institutional life. While the church did on occasion look outside at the world surrounding it, the outward interest and thrust was not the prime interest. The fundamental concern was with the inner life of the congregation, with the church as institution and not with the church as mission. The inward-looking church was described by Gibson Winter: "The introverted church is one which puts its own survival before its mission, its own identity above its task, its internal concerns before its apostolate, its rituals before its ministry."[6] When the church looks inward, it looks at its life of worship and teaching, fellowship and organizational activities, as being all-important.

The movement outward has been radical and therefore upsetting. It has upset especially those people, both clergy and lay, who have felt comfortable with the inward approach. Now they have suddenly been forced to look upon the inward only as a preparation for the outward and, more than that, as justified only by the degree to which it prepares for the outward. This change is threatening, because formerly it was assumed that the inward was the important matter and the outward something peripheral. Now the outward mission alone is emphasized, and the inward life of the church is suspected of serving either as a substitute for or diversion from the outward.

Before trying to indicate what this shift seems to demand of pastor and people, let us also consider the progression from success to service as the criterion.

[6] Gibson Winter, *The Suburban Captivity of the Churches* (Garden City: Doubleday & Company, Inc., 1961), p. 103.

There is no doubt that many ministers as well as laymen have great difficulty making this transition in priorities. We live in a culture where success is worshiped, and the tests of success are clear because they are quantitative. Since this success motif is so much a part of our culture, it is hardly surprising that it is the criterion by which most laymen judge the church. If the statistical picture is not good, then they conclude that something is fundamentally and seriously wrong. If the church is losing members, suffering financial pinches, fading in its standing as a "prestige" congregation, there is much heart searching by laymen who can't understand why those things happen. So, when the success image begins to fade from a congregation, the initial assumption is that the pastoral leadership must be at fault. Likewise many in the pastoral ministry also continue to judge by this success standard. They are often so barren theologically that they have no other way by which to determine the worth of a man's ministry.

As long as this success mania holds sway, we can never come to understand and adopt the service concept. And what makes this especially unfortunate is that we may be heading into a period in which no success stories are likely to be written. The church in America seems quite definitely to be headed for a minority status. We are going to be a remnant people, and our dreams of a populace joyously embracing the faith and entering the church will remain only dreams. We are going to be a minority and we are going to lose members at an increasing rate as tensions mount and as the cozy alliance between church and society is disrupted. This break will come about because it will become clearer and clearer that Christian faith is not simply an echo of the world nor is it merely a culture phenomenon. Being a member of the church will no longer be identified automatically as "a good thing to do." When this realization finally hits the American populace, fewer people will be interested in the church.

This can, of course, be the most liberating moment known by American Christianity for many years. It can free the church from the faithless anxiety about success to take upon itself our Lord's servant ministry. The willingness to attempt this servant ministry is found increasingly in the young pastors of today, but it is not yet found in any like degree among the laity. If pastor and people are going to work in cooperative and supportive fashion, there must be a willingness to serve and to be indifferent about success.

The third progression is a part of this series, but is so important that it deserves separate treatment in the next section of the chapter. It is the progression from the church as supporter of the social order to the church as disturber of the social fabric.

What does this change in understanding about the basic function of the church imply about the roles of pastor and people? Unless the whole enterprise is to go down the drain in a flood of mutual animosity, there must be a recognition of the proper role of the pastor. For too long we have thought of the pastor as the hired man of the congregation. He not only has been expected to carry on the traditional clerical functions, but at a deep and fundamental level he has been considered to be an instrument of the congregation's will. While not always clearly stated, it is often the unspoken assumption (and sometimes the implied threat) that those who hire can direct what is to be done and sometimes what is to be said. If the minister remains content with his traditional role as clergyman, there is no problem. But if he feels himself to be minister of the Word, a word that is a "fire shut up in my bones" (Jeremiah 20:9 RSV), he experiences conflict and his people share it.

The ground rule needed here is tied up with a rediscovery of something we dislike even to mention in Protestantism. It is hard to write about this without being misunderstood; yet this risk must be run, because there can be no validity for the pastoral ministry unless pastor and people come to a new and deeper understanding of the proper meaning of pastoral authority. Since they have suffered from such a terrible inferiority complex in recent years, ministers have laid on the altar of congregational equanimity a decent sense of their own professional competence. They tend to lose sight of the fact that they are men commissioned to seek to discover and then to declare the will of God. This responsibility is an awesome burden and a humbling privilege. But the difficulties involved in knowing the will of God and the perils involved in any attempt to declare it must not be used as excuses by laymen to stifle the attempt, or by pastors to escape the burden of their calling. Fully aware of the temptations which beset him (and so on guard against them) the pastor must be granted the liberty to seek to know and to speak the will of God. This frightful burden can be assumed only when pastor and people together support one another in the attempt, being willing to listen and learn in a mutual effort to discover the will of God.

Although this claim to authority may seem to be arrogant and may appear to be special pleading for a particular profession, the need for such authority is desperate. Moreover, I am convinced that the attempt to meet this need has been frustrated in the past by an unwillingness to face the issues openly and honestly.

However, pastoral authority as a personal matter is not the issue. Any man who is suffering from the desire to exercise power for its own sake has simply not understood at all what the servant ministry means. But pastoral authority sufficient to enable a man to do his task with integrity and satisfaction is very important. Without this authority, ministers will not be able to do what needs to be done. The ultimate reason for stressing this need for authority is for the sake of the Christian mission. This pastoral authority does not mean that the pastor's view on any subject is to be accepted without question as some word from "on high."

Rather, it is the pastor's calling to give himself with real discipline to the Word, to ask what it means for the corporate witness of the people, to ponder and reflect in the light of the Word the forms needed by the church, to give expression to the convictions which seem called for in the situation and — when all this has been done, with all the integrity, courage and insight he can bring to the task — to offer such views for the consideration, correction, and implementation by the people. In an era when few of the laity have the time for this sort of venture, the pastoral responsibility becomes greater than it has ever been.

Langdon Gilkey described the need for pastoral authority with fine sensitivity:

> However, when the church becomes coextensive with the world, when its members receive their dominant ideas — religious and ethical — from their business life, from service club speakers, and from weekly magazines, then a new situation has arisen for authority in the church. Now the voice of the layman reflects in all probability the simple voice of his culture. In this case, if the authority of the minister is felt to arise solely from the congregation and his function is understood to be solely that of serving their needs and meeting their standards, then pulpit and church alike are apt to be less free than under an ecclesiastical hierarchy. . . . Protestantism should seek in our day to recapture its older tradition: that the pulpit, he who stands in it, and so the church as a whole, are first of all servants of the Word, not of the mind of the congregation. It should be emphasized that it is the minister's task and duty to bring the judgment of God as well as the comforts of His grace upon the congregation and its life — especially where they least expect and wish it.[7]

The people need to defend, for the sake of Christian mission, the pastor's right and responsibility to be the servant of the Word. And the pastor must always be aware that while he must be responsive to his people he is ultimately

[7] Langdon B. Gilkey, *How the Church Can Minister to the World Without Losing Itself* (New York: Harper & Row Publishers, Inc., 1964), p. 84.

responsible to God. Even so, the fine line between conviction and arrogance will be lost on many occasions. If arrogance in the pastoral office is scandalous — and I wholeheartedly agree that it is — so is a craven timidity masquerading as a profound piety.

IV

We come now to the other troublesome area of pastor-people tension, represented by the third of the progressions mentioned above: the church moving from supporter of the social order to the church as disturber of the social fabric. The way in which the Christian ministry has been caught up in the swirling currents of social action is part of the revolution of our times. When they are confronted by the spectacle of pastors in picket lines, organizing the poor, demanding civil rights, protesting the governmental policy in Vietnam, laymen rub their eyes and wonder what is going on! It is really not surprising that they feel tossed in many directions, launched on a crazy ride which is not at all what they expected when they became involved in the church. They are no longer sure of much of anything, and the pastor, whom they had thought previously to be a factor of stability in an often turbulent world, turns out to be the very person causing some of the turbulence. So radical is this change that it behooves pastors to be both sympathetic and sensitive toward laymen.

Sympathy and sensitivity, however, cannot be allowed to alter the basic thrust of the ministry in this day. As long as social conditions remain as they are, violating the values of the Christian tradition, the church must move from supporter of the *status quo* to disturber of the social peace. Increasingly, this role of social critic will be seen not as a diversion from the church's task, but as the central task. It is the vocation of the people of God to hurl an everlasting No in the teeth of a complacent establishment which is more intent upon keeping things on an even keel than upon establishing justice and defending human dignity. The church may lose many from its ranks, but the church may also in the process recover its integrity and find what it really means to live under the cross.

At this point we must face the fact that many of the people of the churches are simply not ready to accept this new thrust. It is this unwillingness which creates the "crunch" in which many pastors are now caught. While there has been a great deal written and said about the new laity, most of the discussion seems to be about a very small minority. This new laity has not been discovered in the studies which have been made. Pastor and people are going to be in tension for a long time to come before the laity accepts the role of the church as a disturber of the social peace and the champion of those who are the forgotten and the oppressed of society. Consider, in this connection the plain meaning of Yoshio Fukuyama's study of 8,554 parishioners in 151 local congregations of the United Church of Christ. He summarizes the results of the study:

> They see their minister primarily as a leader of worship, comforter of the sick and bereaved and worker with children and youth. . . . One of the least frequently given reasons for joining the church was because it was a "place to serve others." Church boards were mentioned three times more frequently than social action groups as being very important aspects of the church program. The lowest order of priority was given to the church helping the parishioner to understand "his daily work as a Christian vocation" and to become "aware of the needs of others in my community." . . . There is a wide gulf which separates beliefs from actions.[8]

This study describes not some idealized layman but the actual person in the pews and on the boards of churches. He is a real person and should be given the dignity of being accepted as such.

[8] Yoshio Fukuyama, *The Parishioners: A Sociological Interpretation* (Mimeographed), (New York: United Church Board for Homeland Ministries, 1966), pp. 38-39.

Plainly, in this area of social criticism as in that regarding the basic purpose of the church, the pastor must insist upon his freedom. He must work and hope that the people will see how essential such freedom is to the proper discharge of their calling. This pastoral freedom does not mean that the people must accept whatever is said, for every pastor is human and knows that he can be grievously mistaken many times. He does not ask for automatic agreement, which is virtually a meaningless response. He asks, rather, for a mutual freedom, which grants him the right to speak and the people the right to dissent. This implies a recognition that freedom in the church is a two-way street, involving a freedom of the people as well as a freedom of the pulpit.

At all times, it is the responsibility of the pastor to claim the freedom to seek to discover and declare what the Word implies about the totality of human existence and resist with every power at his command the insidious assertion that he is beyond his proper realm when he talks about poverty and votes and war and civil rights. On the issue of the pastor's right to speak in these areas, no compromise is possible — none at all! Whatever tumult may be caused by this insistence, the risk must be run. Otherwise, although we may be peaceful, we can never dare to claim that we are faithful.

When the pastor ventures into these touchy areas, asking the people to respect the ground rules of his freedom to do so, he also should follow some guiding principles. He must respect the facts. The great trouble with many pastors is their benign assumption that a kind heart can excuse a weak mind. They do not do their hard homework with sufficient integrity. They are professionally addicted to the platitude, and having uttered it, they are suffused with a rosy glow of goodness. If the man in the pulpit is going to speak, and if he expects to be heard on the tough issues of our day, he is going to have to do far more real tough thinking.

The minister must dare the discipline of the specific, refusing to rest in a generality so vague nobody can take exception to it or action upon it.

This requirement of accuracy and specificity does not mean that ministers should be silent because they can't be experts. But before they dare to state what they believe to be God's will in the vexing issues of the day, they ought to have the decency to make sure of their facts, to see that their analysis is as honest as they can make it, to make certain that the alternatives have been thoroughly explored, and to discharge the other requirements which face any man who speaks on such issues.

There is a second principle which should guide the pastor. Care should be exercised that the independence of the church be maintained. Once again we are touching an area where it is very easy to be misunderstood. This book takes its stand, with no apology, with those who believe that the church must be active in the issues of the public sector. It is not possible for the church to be neutral, concerned only with the setting forth of the issues and then saying, in effect, "Take your pick and express yourself wherever you wish." The church, on the contrary, is under the imperative summons to be "the church for others." It must be that institution which seeks to speak for those who have no voice, to champion those for whom no one else cares, to seek justice for the oppressed. Such concerns plainly belong to the church.

At the same time, the church dare not let itself become the captive of any group in modern society. Whether the group is of the left or the right, whether it is black or white, the church must be free to bring the programs and policies of such groups under judgment. If this freedom is not asserted, the church has become the captive church; and its freedom under God has been seriously compromised.

Admittedly, this assertion of freedom isn't a popular position. The church will have to speak against the policies of some groups with whose ultimate goal there is agreement, because fine goals can be frustrated by inept programs. The church can serve the cause of human progress by this kind of careful assessment of all groups and causes. Such assessment cannot be permitted to paralyze the willingness of the church to act, but it may preserve both the church and other groups from tragic blunders. While this strategy will bring the church and pastor into disrepute in many circles, it nevertheless is the only way compatible with a sense of prophetic responsibility.

An important ground rule for pastor and people, easy enough to state in conventional terms but hard to carry out in practice, is reverence for human personality. In order to fulfill the role outlined in this chapter, the minister must always keep a proper balance between arrogance and obsequiousness. Nothing will help him more than an adequate theology which takes seriously the ambiguity of motives at work in all groups and individuals. When the tensions mount and the conflicts arise in the church, the thing that may keep these problems within bounds is a knowledge of the fragility of one's own goodness, a keen sense of the ambiguity of motivation which is part of all human existence. Then it is possible to be kept open and teachable, and the laity from whom one is temporarily divided will not be seen as fiends, intent upon destruction, but fallible beings like oneself, caught in the awful dilemma of a day when no neat and simple choices are possible. Self-righteousness is the force which generates unwholesome conflict. Such a self-righteousness is hard to maintain when one lives with a vivid sense of the gap between one's own course of conduct and the transcendent will of God. This realization is not meant to paralyze the willingness to speak and act; it is meant to guard against a hardness of heart.

Involved in this reverence for personality as a sort of corollary is a scrupulous regard for the right to dissent. The false prophet will always hover over us and sometimes speak through us. We are fallible, and therefore we must be willing to grant to others the right to dissent. Surely, in a day like this the will of God will seldom be revealed by one man from some Olympian height, but rather by all of the people of God, clergy and lay, being ready to hear the Word, to share with one another what they believe that Word implies for our day, and to learn from one another. If we can remain open to each other we shall find that the will of God becomes known in the midst of resolute and responsible wrestling with the life we live, in which we need each other, pastor and people. We find, indeed, our real bond in a common commitment to the word of God. When pastor and people alike live under that Word of judgment and healing, they may experience conflict but never lovelessness.

The church has embarked upon a difficult and precarious course. The ministry of the next few decades will be in for tough going. And for it we are going to need the spirit which shines through the words of a Methodist minister in Ohio. He said, "I took twelve years to make up my mind; or rather I waged a twelve-year battle with God from the time I was called to be a minister until I entered the ministry. The battle was hellish. I lost; I am joyful."

He demonstrates a rare and choice spirit. If the pastoral ministry in the next generation is going to be anything like that which has been sketched in this book, it is obvious that the New Breed will have to be a special group of human beings. What sort of ministry is it going to be and what qualities are necessary for it? To this we turn in our final chapter.

7

BETWEEN THE NO LONGER
AND THE NOT YET

This book has been written in an attempt to convey to others — especially young men now looking for an area of service — a feeling of the zest and excitement which can be known in the pastoral ministry. Despite the perplexities now surrounding it, I have tried to express clearly my conviction that the pastoral ministry remains a challenging, difficult, but tremendously worthwhile vocation. Its day, I believe, is by no means over. Yet I confess I am troubled as I read over the preceding chapters. The picture there presented seems to focus largely on the burdens of the pastoral ministry; the privileges are hard to find. And so I come to the final chapter a bit troubled by a fear that this honest appraisal may turn out to be a discouragement rather than an inducement to enlist some of the keenest young Christians of our day in the pastoral vocation.

Why should any young man enter this profession? He has been told of the widespread questioning of the value of the institutional church. He has been told of the imperative necessity for the church and for pastors to take the chances involved in social activism, with resulting conflicts and tensions which are often devastating in their effects. Furthermore, he has been told of the burden of administrative work under which he will often chafe and about which he will have cause to grumble. Reading this account may evoke the question: Why bother about this vocation? The burdens are there in abundant and clear detail, but where are the privileges?

At this point the answer emerges in the form of paradox. These burdens *are* the privileges. The answer may be puzzling and of little comfort, but it is the only forthright way in which I can put the matter. *The burden is the privilege.* The pastoral vocation should be entered only by those who can understand and live with this paradox. And this will be possible only if pastoral care of congregations can be seen as a response to the love of Christ. The pastorate will be assumed, not because it is easy or comfortable, not because it promises some sort of material reward, not because the pastor is likely to be venerated by the community; but only because it is understood to be a strategically important place for a man whose life has been claimed at a deep level by Christ and who therefore seeks a servant ministry. In the phrase made popular by Dietrich Bonhoeffer, he is content to be, like his Lord, "a man for others." He finds this burden to be his privilege.

Obviously, this view of the pastoral ministry requires a rare spirit in men. This final chapter must attempt to state what the ministry is going to be like in the future and what style of life, what manner of men, are needed to fulfill this type of ministry.

I

No matter how poignant it may be, nostalgia for yesterday's form of ministry will not provide an authentic form for today's need. The truth of this statement should be obvious. We have been told, almost to the point of boredom, that we live in a revolutionary age and that the spirit of rebellion has touched every aspect of modern existence with a disturbing impact. The church has not been exempt from this spirit of the times; we have tried to look at some aspects of the mood in these pages. Therefore, within the setting of this revolutionary age we must seek a valid form of ministry.

Unfortunately, however, what should be apparent is frequently quite different from what is actually understood. There is a strong current of nostalgia running in modern Protestantism. A great many Protestants feel keenly that they live in a world they never made, and many of its aspects they thoroughly detest. While there are some features of modernity which they can accept with joy, there are others to which they are passively indifferent or bristlingly antagonistic.

Since these people have been uprooted by rapid change, they feel threatened by whatever disrupts their ties to a known and familiar past. In many ways, the church functioned to give this sense of a linkage to that past; it was part of rural or small-town society, remembered with greater fondness as it fades more and more into the misty past. Many Protestants, whether ministers or lay people, have never really come to terms with the urban setting. They have had to accept it as a fact, but this grudging acknowledgment is quite different from accepting it as a good thing. A rural or a small-town society is still the real ideal of the people of many of our churches and, whether admitted or not, is the ideal of many clergymen. While we may live physically in a jet age, we live emotionally in a Currier and Ives time. This rural America was *the* Protestant America. It was a relaxed America, although never as good as nostalgia makes it seem. The frantic speed-up associated with the technological revolution had not occurred. The deadly depersonalization of modern existence was not known. Above all, America had not yet become so predominantly an urban civilization. The city has long been — and still is — the unsolved problem for the Protestant community. With the rise of the city there has been the gradual development of an entirely new setting for Christian witness. Instead of being a predominantly Protestant nation, the United States is today a pluralistic society, forcing clergymen and laymen to adjust their thinking in a radical fashion. In somewhat cumbersome terms, it has become an urban, post-Protestant America. And many do not like it very much.

What has been quickly outlined here has now become the unquestioned analysis of most of Protestantism's thoughtful adherents. What remains to be done is to let this analysis of Protestantism's setting become part of the thinking of more of those in the ministry and an increasing number of the laity. This task is still before us, because many have been unable or unwilling to look honestly at what has happened in this land.

A strange aspect of this total situation is that the desire to turn back the clock affects particularly religion. The man who wants his religion to be the same sort of faith he knew as a boy would resist strenuously any suggestion that we get rid of some of the technological innovations by which life has been made easier. Everything is to be up-to-date except his religion, which is his one source of contact with a past that he doesn't want to reestablish, yet is unwilling to let go completely.

A basic assumption needs, then, to be made at this point. We neither can nor should seek to re-create the past Protestant period. In addition to the fact that such an effort is a quixotic impossibility, it is also a failure in faithfulness. Each age of Christian history has called for a ministry valid in a particular setting. Ministry, as part of the life of the Christian church in every age, is a continuing necessity; the *form* of ministry can and must be changed to fit the different conditions of a new day. The meaning of faithfulness in ministry is in part a willingness to risk something in the search for a valid form of ministry for one's own day.

As an act of faith, the present generation of ministers and those who will be entering the ministry in the near future need to reject the lure of nostalgia. This rejection of nostalgia does not mean a cavalier dismissal of the past, as though it had nothing to teach us and all wisdom arrived with our generation. Gratitude to the past is always in order, but bondage to it never is. And it is this bondage which must be broken.

If I read the signs with any accuracy, it is clear that we are confronted by two movements within the ranks of present and potential parish ministers. One is a movement backward, a panicky attempt to renew the church by recapturing the best of the past. The other is a movement outward which is an abandonment of the pastoral enterprise itself. Both movements have been produced by the same set of factors. The movement for church renewal can accomplish at best only a part of what is desired. Accordingly, some will say that since so little has been done, they can no longer stay within the institution; others will say that since the whole effort of renewal has achieved so little, it is clear that renewal was never the answer. At the same time that there is this assessment of church renewal there will be an equally melancholy evaluation of the movement toward social reform. The same type of verdict is likely to emerge: much hoped for, little accomplished. And again the same response will be made: some will abandon the church as an agency of social reform, and others will contend that the failure makes it perfectly clear that this was an inappropriate role for the church to have adopted.

In this difficult climate of opinion the men must be found for the ministry of tomorrow.

II

If the form of ministry cannot be found in yesterday, and if there is no clear and compelling idea of what a relevant ministry might be for today, we are as a result in an interim period. The Ecumenical Institute of Chicago put this fact vividly in a sentence in one of its publications: "The wedge blade of the future is forged by those who stand between the no longer and the not yet, laying down their lives for the sake of all men." The phrase captures succinctly the nature of our situation. We are at that point where old forms no longer win assent or show vitality, and where new forms have not yet proved themselves with sufficient clarity to claim our commitment. The ministry in this generation and, even more, the ministry of the next generation is going to be carried on in this murky region between the no longer and the not yet.

The biblical image of the ministry for tomorrow is that of the Exodus. From the settled life of Egypt, where things moved in accustomed if restrictive grooves, to the demanding freedom of the wilderness is the pilgrimage of the ministry. And let there be no mistake; the wilderness is not an easy place in which to minister. There are no familiar trails, no precisely defined duties. A particular spirit of adventure is required to be willing and able to carry on a ministry which is a matter of frequent improvisation, altering courses to meet new needs, abandoning cherished procedures because they no longer are effective.

It is becoming clearer all the time that the wilderness is the locale of ministry from now into the foreseeable future. For the minister of today and tomorrow the wilderness must be accepted as the Promised Land with rejoicing. J. C. Hoekendijk has put this clearly:

> Let us not have any illusions, the way toward the world of tomorrow leads into the desert. I believe that the Biblical story of the exodus will, in a very special way, become our story — even if the outcome is different. Disappointments and setbacks await us, but they are surrounded by a host of signs and miracles. In the drought we shall find an oasis, indeed also Mara, bitter water. . . . Where now we only vaguely and uncertainly detect a track, there will be a path clearly shown to us. What happens along the way

will not be so conspicuous. Nothing for the newspapers. Here and there a sign of shalom: reconciliation, peace, joy, freedom. . . . And in these signs we shall see the future approach: the Lord, who comes toward us and who, according to his promise, will make the desert into the Promised Land.[1]

This is the kind of setting in which ministry will be carried on, and this is the faith needed for the venture.

The concerns at which we have looked in this book are not by any means finished. We are on the way; the church has become, in a very real sense, once again a pilgrim community. The pain involved in this process is real, for it is hard to cast aside cherished ways and structures. Nor is it comfortable to be forever on the move, always ready to strike the tent and find other ground. It is understandable that there should be a desire to stay put for a while, to claim some territory as one's own, and to put down roots. While this mood can be sympathetically understood, it would be poor strategy to offer any hope that such staying put will be possible.

Very quickly, let me indicate some possible directions for the church. Assuming that the concern for renewal of the church remains strong, certain consequences must follow. There will continue to be a need for prophetic self-criticism by those in the church against *the church as it is*. Without this continuing judgment, the church grows complacent and ceases to be the community whose existence is shaped by the Word. Many of the existing forms and structures will have to be either radically changed or completely cast aside. The shape of denominationalism must increasingly be subjected to a rigorous scrutiny, which demands that denominationalism justify itself in terms of Christian mission. The activities and priorities of local congregations

[1] J. C. Hoekendijk, *The Church Inside Out*, Isaac C. Rottenberg, trans. (Philadelphia: The Westminster Press, 1964), pp. 188-189. Copyright © by J. C. Hoekendijk, 1964. Eng. trans. copyright © 1966, by W. L. Jenkins. Used by permission.

must constantly be evaluated in terms of this same basic criterion of mission. A ruthless pruning, getting rid of everything which does not justify itself in terms of preparing the people of God for mission, must be carried on.

Consequently the minister can't settle down into a comfortable assurance that his role and that of the church are clear to himself, to the people of the congregation, and to the community as a whole. These roles will probably not be clear to anyone, and he will therefore be engaged throughout his ministry in a continuous process of trying this, trying that, retaining this, throwing out that, all of it a constant process of endeavoring to find forms and structures which will most effectively help in a ministry of reconciliation. Many times the sheer chaos of this sort of effort will threaten to overwhelm both pastor and church. The crisis of ministerial identity and the equally severe crisis of church morale are likely to be continuous accompaniments of ministry in this day.

The difficulty of the enterprise cannot be overemphasized. The possibility of mistakes will be present at every point along the way. Some new enterprises have already proved foolish; they simply did not fulfill their promise. Many of them have passed from the scene. Some old structures have proved very hard to destroy or change. Hands have been raised in horror at some of the new experiments and in defense of established ways of doing things. Both clergy and laity often feel that they are being tossed wildly around, and many in both groups wonder if all the effort is really worth the cost.

The task of change and renewal will take a heavy toll. While one venture is being evaluated, another must be made ready. And all along the way there is the spectre of sheer exhaustion on one side and cynical abandonment of the venture on the other.

If there are difficulties in a ministry carried on between the no longer and the not yet, there are also advantages;

these should not be forgotten. There is a quality of excitement which ministry did not always have in the past. There is the chance to share in the shaping of a proper response on the part of the Christian community to a new day and its demands. There is freedom from the heavy hand of the past and the chance to work out appropriate responses for the present and future. In short, an age in which new things are being done on all sides has its counterpart in a church which is waking out of its slumber and getting ready to meet the modern world on its own ground. For the minister the next decades can be a zestful period indeed.

Not only will we live between the no longer and the not yet in terms of church renewal, but also in terms of social activism. We have already touched on this matter in this book. It needs to be put in the picture here, too, because it is a central fact of church existence. It is somewhat difficult, I confess, to know what is likely to be the final result of all our social effort. Here one's basic optimism or pessimism will cloud the picture. Without trying to be dogmatic about it, we can at least indicate certain possibilities.

The possibility must be faced that the lack of any really clear victories will send the minister and the church from social involvement. Recoiling from the worldly involvement because it seemed to accomplish so little, some men will be strongly tempted to turn once again inward. They will conclude that society, no matter how valiant man's efforts, will remain finally a scene of frustration. They will decide that the proper sphere for the church is the inward life of man — his relation to God, his personal problems, his family life. Regretfully they will retreat to the private sphere as the place where religion seems able to function, assuming that the public issues are simply beyond the power of religion to shape.

How strong this mood is likely to be cannot be known. There are so many imponderables. If social action can point to no significant victories, the mood of retreat will be strong indeed. If, however, there are significant victories (for example, the end of war in Vietnam, the termination of the draft, the beginning of real attack on the slums, the achievement of some real progress in racial relations), then the mood of defeat would be far less powerful. For at least some now in the ministry and for most of those termed the New Breed, ministry without social action is inconceivable.

The "crunch" mentioned in the *Life* article cited in a previous chapter will get fiercer. Some of the current attacks on the church's involvement in so-called political areas will mount in intensity. As a result, many congregations will be filled with strife and contention. It will take a hardy breed to stand up under this kind of pressure, involving not only vocational futures but family welfare and all the rest of the factors involved. The picture would be pleasant if the pastoral ministry could deal simply with the rewarding and delightful experiences which are, fortunately, always part of it — the privilege of ministry to people at times of joy and sorrow, the sharing in the problems of all sorts and conditions of men, the effort to help people to find sustaining faith in a demanding day. But while these things are part of the pastoral ministry, it would be less than honest not to point out that even these aspects are often threatened by the pastor's social involvement. Indeed, one of the heaviest burdens many pastors have to carry is that of knowing that social action on behalf of some persons frustrates his pastoral work with other persons. Because this book is not intended to be a sentimental celebration of the pastorate, but rather an accurate description of the situation, this fact of opposition to the pastor's social activism must be recorded as part of church life in modern America.

This problem may finally force us into an entirely new type of ministry. The ministry, in order to establish sufficient independence of action, may have to become again a "tent-making ministry." The pastor may no longer be dependent upon the congregation for his livelihood. An adaptation of the French worker-priest experiment may be needed. Some form of ministry, we have insisted, is going to be a necessity for the Christian community; but no particular form is sacred and to be kept from all change.

Thus far in this chapter I have simply been trying to say that the form of tomorrow's ministry cannot be found in yesterday; nostalgia is no answer. Furthermore, I have tried to indicate the peculiar nature of ministry in a time between the no longer and the not yet.

III

This new kind of ministry in the local church will not appeal to everybody, even those committed to the Christian enterprise. Nor should it. The need will continue for men who will see their form of vocational obedience in terms of participating in many of the new extra-parochial ministries. These men must be seen fully as ministers and supported with interest and concern by those in the churches. As the body has many members (in the Pauline figure) so the church in this day has to have many different forms of ministry. There are no lower or higher orders, no better or worse forms; there is a ministry of Christ which takes on many different forms in this day and age.

Those who see the pastoral ministry as a fitting response for them will have to possess special qualities. A strong sense of vocation will have to be part of the spirit of such men. This vocation must be rooted and grounded in the call of God.

A great deal of mischief has been done by our emphasis upon the call of God. It has sometimes been made into a quasi-magical operation, whereby God in a direct and miraculous way laid his hand upon a certain individual. Other times, it has been interpreted as a matter of some mysterious hearing of a voice. The net result has been that many men, surely called authentically by God, have not recognized the call because it did not come to them in these prescribed and stereotyped ways. These men have thus been lost to the pastoral ministry.

What is needed is not less emphasis upon ministry as vocation, but a better understanding of what the call really means. We should know by now that God deals with us in terms of our situations. He calls through a variety of means. Involved is a sense of the importance of the Christian enterprise, a confidence in the truth of the gospel. There can be no vocation in the Christian sense of the term without these convictions. In addition, one must assess his own gifts and capacities, using every available means to determine these. When this has been done, it is necessary to ask how these gifts and talents can be most effectively used for the sake of the Christian mission. For one man this may mean a so-called secular vocation. For another it may mean enlistment in one of the new forms of ministry. And for some it will mean the pastoral ministry in the local church.

This understanding of vocation will free it from the trappings of some mysterious enterprise foreign to most men in this day and age. Let it be emphasized, however, that this understanding does not render the pastorate any less the call of God; nor does it make any less important for the man in pastoral ministry the conviction that his particular sphere of service is where God wishes him to be. Note carefully those words: where God wishes him to be; the place of service is not always where the person might wish to be. Given the analysis of the pastoral ministry undergirding this book, the conclusion is inescapable that many men would not wish such ministry to be the place where they are to serve.

Denis de Rougemont has put clearly the meaning of vocation as sketched out here:

To follow one's vocation, contrary to what is generally believed, is not to follow one's inclination (even uphill), but to be swept in spite of oneself toward goals and into an action to which nothing whatever inclines us. *I am the man least suited for this!* groans the individual, when an unknown force, wrenching him from himself, flings him upon his *persona.* . . . His effectiveness is born of this surrender, of this condign defeat unremittingly inflicted upon the natural individual by what is not him, but which comes to *summon* him and creates him forever.[2]

To be created in the act of accepting vocation is a possibility faith holds out for a man.

The type of person needed for the pastoral ministry is the inner-directed person of David Riesman's familiar analysis. He said that there are three different personality types — the tradition-directed who finds his opinions formed and his conduct shaped by the force of the past; the other-directed person who takes his cues for opinion and conduct from the people around him — his is the conformist character; and the inner-directed person who possesses those resources of insight and character which enable him to determine his opinions and shape his conduct without complete dependence upon tradition and without determination by the opinions of others. Riesman contended that this third personality type had been produced by a particular epoch and in all probability is on its way out. In terms of the need set forth here, however, it is clear that the pastoral ministry needs men of this third type if the Christian mission is to recover its integrity.

We have been concerned to emphasize that the past cannot be the sole source of a form for ministry. Nor can the form of ministry be defined by others, because the fact must be honestly faced that the laity of the churches have not been able to achieve sufficient emancipation from cultural surroundings to think of ministry in terms derived from

[2] Denis de Rougemont, *Dramatic Personages,* Richard Howard, trans. (New York: Holt, Rinehart & Winston, Inc., 1964), p. 116.

faith itself. Hence the task of determining a form for ministry must be accepted as the responsibility largely of the ministry. Obviously, the time must come when this responsibility is shared with and accepted by the laity; but it would be, I am convinced, unreal folly to wait until the laity can work out this problem. The working out of the form of ministry by the men engaged in the enterprise day by day will be another aspect of the loneliness of the vocation.

IV

If the minister can resist the lure of nostalgia, accepting the fact that ministry now must find new forms and procedures; if he can undergird his effort with a strong sense of vocation; if he is willing to live in a sort of time between the times and find satisfaction in the chance to shape the emerging forms — if he can do these things, the pastoral ministry will be a challenging and satisfying sphere of service. But even this kind of commitment will not be enough. A basic necessity is a tough theology which will enable the pastor to avoid the traps that lurk in the way.

Somehow the theology needed for pastoral ministry must be one which can take into its scope the empirical reality of the people and the institution. It is always tempting to deal with abstractions. In working out new concepts of ministry, one easily loses sight of the fact that the congregation is made up of flesh-and-blood persons. These persons need to be seen in the full reality of their humanity. While it is important always to think in terms of theological symbols, as we have done frequently in the pages of this book, it is also important to keep constantly before us the real persons. Otherwise, we simply deal with abstractions, not with realities; and we are apt to become disillusioned because reality and symbol stand in such glaring contradiction.

Langdon Gilkey provides a helpful caution at this point. He notes that in many treatises about the church

[it] is described, not as if it were composed of finite and sinful men and women living in a particular cultural environment and in some sort of relation to God, but as if the church were made up entirely of biblical symbols — as if "koinonia," "People of God," "lordship of Christ," and so on, were the elements that together make up the church. Now, while in theology it may be appropriate to speak of God solely in the language of biblical and perhaps philosophical symbols, it is extremely dubious whether it is meaningful or accurate to speak of a concrete historical institution made up of visible people exclusively in such symbolic, biblical terms.[3]

It is, I think, worse than dubious. From the point of view of the functioning of the pastor, such abstraction contributes to a disillusionment with people and with the church.

One of the real needs of the man in the pastoral ministry is a theology which leads him to an understanding of human beings and to a capacity to accept them as they are. Part of the trouble with speaking in abstract terms like "holy nation" or others is that the contrast between what such phrases assume and the reality of the actual lives of the people of the church is so glaring. The result often is that the people are dismissed as hopeless, and more often than we like to admit, a subtle feeling of spiritual superiority works its way into the pastor. He rejects the people out of some supposed spiritual greatness in himself.

The starting point of an answer to this problem is a wholesome sense of the pastor's constant sharing in the sinfulness of human nature. If a man can develop a theology of such honesty that he knows himself as a sinner, he is not quite so likely to grow disenchanted with the people of the church. Besides enabling him to demonstrate a humility which is always healthy, this attitude would have the additional merit of uniting pastor and people in a common ac-

[3] Gilkey, *op. cit.*, p. 134.

knowledgment of sin. Out of such an awareness there may spring an openness and humility which will moderate some of the tensions that are bound to be part of church life in the next few decades. If both pastor and people recognize that they are not altogether righteous, they may also be able to maintain a fellowship with one another which will make possible the continuation of the search for valid ways of Christian living.

This sort of theology can help to avoid the perils of pietism. Pietism has always been a snare for people of real sincerity in religion. Believing that the church has made too many compromises, they feel that they can no longer remain within the familiar structures. So the pietists leave and form a group of congenial and like-minded perfectionists. The old pietism, of course, was appalled by the supposed worldliness of the church which had, they believed, entered into too many alliances with the world, and its members failed to reflect any sort of conduct different from that of the people around them. What needs to be seen is that there is a new pietism today. We have the spectacle of a group of people forming underground churches, leaving the established congregations for a variety of reasons, and setting up small groups of their own. Within these small groups they then carry on what they regard as the essential matter — theological study, social action, or whatever. The old and the new pietism have in common only a slightly self-righteous appraisal of the people of the conventional congregations and a marked similarity of outlook and approach.[4]

The task before us is admittedly a very difficult one; its complete fulfillment may be beyond us. I am not pleading for the sort of theology which despairs of man's ability to do anything, a faithless exulting in sinfulness. But I am asking for a realistic sense of human limitation, so that our

[4] For the perils of contemporary pietism, see my article, "The New Pietism," *The Pulpit*, January, 1968, pp. 8-9.

quest is not for a perfectionism which is unattainable but for a constant effort to grow, to mature, to develop in Christ. Plainly, this kind of approach calls for a balance that is incredibly difficult to achieve. We cannot sit back content with what we are and with what we are doing; that would be fatal. Yet neither can we become so disgusted with ourselves or others that we give up all effort. We must be enabled to confess our unprofitableness and as accepted sinners go back to our tasks.

By this sort of alternation between action and confession we need to live in the church. We do not presume that we are perfect or that perfection is required of us. We do not look upon ourselves as powerless or without any goodness. We know what we are — people with the usual quota of sins and shortcomings. We know whose we are — persons accepted by God despite our sins and shortcomings and summoned to serve him. The realization of our sin keeps us from self-righteousness. The knowledge of God's forgiveness keeps us from despair. Together, I suggest, they equip us for ministry in the church side by side with others who share this same commitment.

But this theology gives the man in the pastoral ministry one other assurance badly needed just now. We have noted in this book the impatient and strident voices telling us how faithless the church is, how irrelevant it has become, how inward-looking its life is, and all the rest of the familiar catalog. What these changes add up to is for some a total abandonment of the church and a conclusion that God cannot use the church as a means for the accomplishment of his will. Strangely enough, however, some of these same critics have no doubts at all about God's use of some of the structures of the secular order for the doing of his will. Theirs is a strange theology, in which there is great confidence in God's ability to use secular structures but none at all in his ability to use the church. While I am quite convinced that we should be cautious about assuming that the church is automatically responsive to God's will, I am also quite convinced that it is singularly inappropriate for us to become so dogmatic about what God can and cannot do in using a variety of institutions, agencies, and structures for the accomplishment of his purpose. It is at least a real possibility that the existing congregations can be used. Indeed, it is clearly evident that such institutions are being used by God. While they may not be as adequate as they should be, they are not completely outside the scope of God's purpose.

The time has come for us to take a closer look at our confident baptizing of the secular realm, as though it were the only arena in which God is to be found, and our equally confident dismissal of the church, as though it were the one arena where God could not be found. We have celebrated the secular and disparaged the church. Now we have come to the time when a new and critical look needs to be taken at the secular.

Basic to all that I have said in this book is a conviction that the Christian faith has a validity which can claim the assent of the man of today. The exciting days of Christian mission are ahead of us, not behind us. But if this excitement is to be experienced and if the promise of these turbulent days is to be realized, we must find pastors for local congregations who will share the new thrust of the church toward mission in the public sector. Essential in this thrust is the recognition that this mission in the world makes more imperative than ever before the careful training of the men and women who must carry on such a ministry. What is surprising today is that so many have been imbued with zeal for Christian witness without really knowing what is Christian about it. As Albert C. Outler has put it:

> The sin for which we may not be forgiven (since we are so far unrepentant of it!) is that, in such a time and amidst all the heroic struggles to make the Christian message relevant to a world in convulsion, we have despised, as indoctrination, the task of ground-

ing the people in our churches in the substance of historic Christianity. It could scarcely be more ironic that just when we have come to be so clear and emphatic about the urgency of the Church's "witness" in and to the world, more and more Christians know less and less about the historic content of that "witness." [5]

To share in the task of developing this kind of understanding and commitment is the task of the pastor.

It is clear that we are in a day of vast and sweeping changes. From the imperative of change the church is by no means exempt. Whatever changes occur, as God seeks to create a church for mission, it is my conviction that local congregations of believers will continue to exist. Such congregations are now here; they provide a group of people already committed to the gospel. What now needs to be done is to work from within these congregations, clergymen and laymen together, in such a fashion that each unit becomes a congregation in mission. This is the task which confronts the next generation of men who see the pastoral ministry as a challenging field of service.

"And these were his gifts: some to be apostles, some prophets, some evangelists, some pastors and teachers . . ." (Ephesians 4:11, NEB). If the Christian mission is to be effective today and tomorrow, there must be "some pastors and teachers."

[5] Albert C. Outler, *Who Trusts in God* (New York: Oxford University Press, 1968), p. 18.

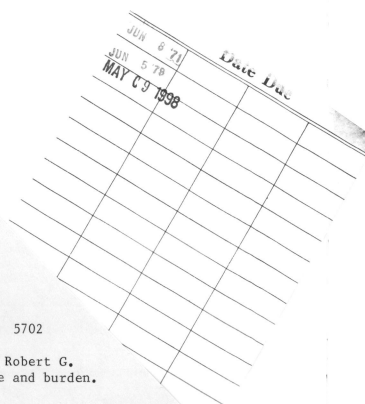